Teaching

f

Garcia ~~Soc.~~

AUTHOR

Teaching Diverrstity

TITLE

C H ☒ ☒

Phi Delta Kappa Educational Foundation
Bloomington, Indiana
U.S.A.

Cover design by Victoria Voelker

Library of Congress Catalog Card Number 98-66870
ISBN 0-87367-807-9
Copyright © 1998 by Ricardo L Garcia
Bloomington, Indiana U.S.A.

In Memory of

Walter Brunet
Beverly Caperton
Hazel Durham

Table of Contents

Introduction 1

Chapter One
Democracy, Diversity, and Universal Education 5
   The Nature of a Free Society 6
   The Role of Universal Education 9
   Schools as Communities 14

Chapter Two
Identifying and Understanding Diversity Issues 19
   Labels and Describing Diversity 20
   Cultures as Frameworks for Understanding 21
   Language Development 25
   Socioeconomic Status 27
   Stigma and Resistance 31
   Learning Style Preferences 34
   Gender Identity and Sexual Orientation 38
   Race and Ethnicity 42
   Religion 45
   Summary 47

Chapter Three
Instructional Strategies that Accommodate Diversity 51
   Safety and Equality 52
   Theoretical Bases for Integration Strategies 55
   Facilitative Teaching in Action 61
   Behavior Management 64
   Critical Thinking 68
   Cross-Cultural Interaction 77
   Summary 84

Chapter Four

Developing Curricula that Reflect Diversity 87
Construction of Knowledge 88
Cultural Literacy 90
Curricula for Cultural Literacy 92
Four Approaches to Teaching for Cultural Literacy 96
Choosing Curricular Materials 99
Student-Created Curricula 107

Chapter Five

Teaching Students to Live in a Diverse Society 111
Socialization and Diversity 112
From Medieval Village to Global Village 113
Socialization in Action 116
Teaching Collaboration 121
Conflict Resolution 123
Conclusion 131

References 135

About the Author 141

Introduction

In August 1973 I began my career as a teacher educator in an institute designed for classroom teachers whose public schools were undergoing desegregation. During a discussion a white teacher asked, "What's the best way to teach black students?" As moderator, I looked to the other teachers. An African-American teacher turned the question around: "Let me ask you, what's the best way to teach a white student?" Everyone laughed — out of anxiety. The white teacher responded, "There is no one best way to teach white students. They are all different." As the white teacher spoke, she realized that she had answered her own question. All students are individuals; there is no one right way to teach all of them.

Thus commenced my quest to address teaching for diversity. Many educators struggle with how to teach today's students to live in a diverse society as effective citizens of the larger community without doing injustice to their individual identities. That goal is the subject of this book, but it is not the only — or even the first — goal. Before teachers can teach their students to live in a diverse society, they must embrace and engage the diversity within their classrooms. Therefore, this book has a dual focus: both teaching diverse students and teaching students to deal positively with diversity.

To sharpen this focus, I have attempted to integrate three broad themes. The first is a way to view the role of the teacher. Teaching for diversity requires that teachers help students to learn by accepting personal responsibility for making meaning. This facilitative teaching is based on constructivist principles that operate from the belief that humans dislike disorder and will organize ideas to make sense of them. Constructivism and facilitative teaching draw from a number of antecedents, including the work of Johann Pestalozzi (1746-1827), Maria Montessori (1870-1952), and John Dewey (1859-1952). All of these educators believed that teaching and learning were best accomplished by finding ways of releasing the student's natural curiosity.

Second is a developmental view of human diversity. I think of human diversity as variations on a theme — permutations and rearrangements of the basic elements that make every person unique. Too often, diversity is regarded as deviations from a sup-posed norm. This view means that some individuals are seen by others as "substandard," "deficient," or "abnormal," perhaps to be tolerated but not to be fully accepted. I believe, on the contrary, that diversity represents variations on the common theme of humanity. Each person displays individual characteristics that, taken together, form the whole fabric of human existence. No thread in this fabric is "better" than another, though they may be different colors, different textures, and so on.

The third theme embodies a set of seven guiding principles that can help educators to teach for diversity. Simply and directly stated to teachers, these principles are as follows:

- Know yourself and how you respond to experiences with diversity.
- Study human differences and examine your attitudes toward them.
- Identify your own and your students' learning styles and work to accommodate different modes of learning.
- Teach critical thinking in the context of cultural awareness.
- Teach self-control, self-respect, and respect for others.
- Foster a positive school and classroom environment — a community of learners.
- Select curricula and instructional materials that exemplify a value for diversity.

This book is arranged into five chapters. Chapter One, which I have titled Democracy, Diversity, and Universal Education, lays a philosophical foundation. To be fully effective, universal education must balance unity and diversity in order to achieve the enduring promise of a free, democratic society. Chapter Two, Identifying and Understanding Diversity Issues, describes diversity by identifying key categories of characteristics evident in student populations. Imbedded in each category are issues that teachers must address both personally and professionally.

Chapter Three, Instructional Strategies that Accommodate Diversity, provides specific, practical information to help teachers facilitate student learning. I give particular attention to teaching students self-assessment and self-management skills, critical thinking skills, and skills for cross-cultural communication.

Chapter Four, Developing Curricula that Reflect Diversity, is aimed at providing ways of looking at what is taught from a perspective of multicultural awareness. School curricula need to reflect the cultural heritages of the total population, the roots of all, not merely of those present in a given classroom. Finally, in Chapter Five, Teaching Students to Live in a Diverse Society, I describe the classroom as a microcosm of society writ large. When classrooms become exemplars for the world outside, then students can better prepare to work and live in a diverse, democratic society.

In writing this book, the main audience that I have kept in mind is classroom teachers at all levels, principally those working in the United States and Canada. I apologize in advance to my Canadian colleagues if I have misrepresented any aspect of Canadian cultures or education. But in too many cases American education has not looked beyond its borders. And so I have attempted, albeit in a relatively small way, to cast a wider vision. I would suggest that American educators can learn much from their counterparts in other areas of the world, and drawing on a Canadian perspective is, at least, a step in a positive direction.

Chapter One

DEMOCRACY, DIVERSITY, AND UNIVERSAL EDUCATION

E pluribus unum — "Out of many, one" — is an expression both of diversity and of unity. The phrase implies that the strength of our nation is founded on the melding of diverse groups and individuals into a unified people: Americans. The phrase and the concept are the keystone of American democracy — indeed of democracy writ large. The United States and Canada share a similar diversity, historically having drawn their populations from immigrant peoples of many origins. For both countries, the survival of democracy has required a weaving together of diverse individual histories and cultural heritages into the unifying fabric of nationhood.

Individual freedom is the hallmark of democratic societies. Such freedom often is expressed in the plural: Americans and Canadians exercise a number of freedoms, such as the freedom of religion and the freedom of speech. The essence of these freedoms, however, is the freedom to be "different" — to hold individual beliefs and to express individual opinions that do not necessarily conform to prevailing or dominant ideas in the society.

This is not to say that there are no societal norms. Unrestrained freedom is chaos. The true value of *e pluribus unum* rests with the

5

willingness of a nation's citizens to find common ground — and common respect for differences. The common ground, translated into norms of behavior, balances a value of difference, or individuality, with a value of social (hence national) unity. A civil society founded on the precepts of democracy, therefore, balances the freedom to be different with the obligation to conform to certain norms.

How, then, should teachers teach for diversity? How should they strike this necessary balance in the classroom? The purpose of this chapter is to discuss a philosophical foundation for teaching for diversity that draws on three concepts: the nature of a free society, the role of universal education, and schools as communities.

The Nature of a Free Society

Free societies are naturally discordant, and social order always is a concern. U.S. Supreme Court Justice Oliver Wendell Holmes once characterized the free society as "messy business." Similarly, institutions based on free expression and free association invariably reverberate with debate and dissension, as individual opinions, needs, and desires clash in the open forum of ideas. Such is necessarily the case in the schools of a democracy.

While dissenters from the prevailing thought-stream are not always honored, in a free society the citizenry is obligated to tolerate the expression of their ideas. Indeed, new ideas often emerge from dissent to become dominant over time. The "progress" of the nation is fueled by the untidy interplay and creative tensions of daily life. Nothing is more powerful than an idea whose time has come. In the 1910s the idea whose time had come was women's suffrage; in the 1960s it was black civil rights. Some would argue that when we look back at the 1990s it will have been gay civil rights.

Conflict, therefore, is not merely inevitable. It is necessary. But no society, however free, can allow civil "messiness" to dissolve the bond of national unity. The glue of social unity — of nationhood — is civility. For the most part, civility is neither written into law nor expressed as explicit rules. Rather, civility is deeply embedded in the folkways and mores of democratic living. It serves as the conflict-resolution mechanism of social order. And it permeates the law without being "the law." Thus civility provides the ethos for a free society — a consensual reciprocity by which individuals respect the rights of others in order that they may pursue their own interests. That is, they allow themselves to be constrained in order to be free — or, at least, relatively free.

Education for freedom must be translated, as Dewey translated it, into the freedom of individual thought and belief. Dewey said:

> The only freedom that is of enduring importance is freedom of intelligence . . . freedom of observation and of judgment exercised in behalf of purposes that are intrinsically worthwhile. (1938, p. 69)

Freedom of intelligence is the freedom in a democratic society to think, feel, and behave in ways that enable individuals to achieve the hopes and dreams that they hold dear — as long as those aspirations do not trammel the individual freedoms of others. To particularize this notion of freedom of intelligence, consider the issue of an "official" language, or languages, in education. How does the language of instruction affect individual freedom as balanced against a societal norm?

In Canada the 1982 *Charter of Rights and Freedoms* guarantees English-speaking and French-speaking parents that their children can be instructed in either official language. Each Canadian province may apply the bilingual policy as it sees fit in order to serve its citizens. However, in the Quebec schools, children are *required* to be educated in French. This practice has antagonized some parents — especially immigrant parents — who, according to their interpretation of the *Charter,* should be allowed to choose either French or English as the language for their children's schooling.

Some would argue that the language policy in Quebec restricts (or, at least, affects) freedom of intelligence and runs counter to Canada's overall policies of multiculturalism. It allows a dominant language (French) to be an exclusive language — tacitly excluding non-speakers. The Quebec policy thereby may limit access to learning by non-French-speaking students. According to the national philosophy, Canadian schools in all provinces should work to enhance the cultural traditions of all groups, including new immigrants, regardless of their language. But, as of this writing, the tension between Canada's aspirations as a multicultural nation and Quebec's adherence to a French-language schooling tradition have not been resolved to everyone's satisfaction. Individual freedom and a societal norm are out of balance.

In the United States, for another example, there is a growing cultural gap between students and the teachers who are trained to teach them. According to the National Council for the Accreditation of Teacher Education (1996, p. 4), many schools are in demographic denial. Minority student enrollments are increasing rapidly. Already 31% of all U.S. public school students come from minority backgrounds. In some states (for example, California) more than 50% of the students come from minority groups. At the same time, only 13% of the teaching force comes from minority groups. And only 5% of the college students studying to become teachers are from minority backgrounds.

Yet another example: Theoretically, 10% of students (more visibly at the secondary school level) may be gay or lesbian. Yet openly gay teachers, who might serve as positive role models for such youth, often are drummed out of the profession for reasons unrelated to their competence as teachers. And openly gay or lesbian college students are discouraged from pursuing education careers or are actively counseled out.

These are examples of societies striving to find the balance point on troublesome issues — issues in which concerned individuals have a legitimate stake in the outcome, but also issues in which the democratic society has a stake in maintaining a level of unity, in finding a common ground.

Teachers are caught in the crossfire over issues regarding race, culture, language, religious beliefs, sex, sexual orientation, and other "differences" that define or identify groups and individuals. Teachers not only must identify these issues, they also must understand the various viewpoints, both individual and societal, and then respond in ways that affirm the values of freedom, unity, and civility. Teachers must engage in professional dialogue that transcends personal beliefs (and prejudices), both in dealing with the issues as they arise in the classroom among their students and in the instructional context of helping students learn how to deal with the same kinds of issues when they arise outside the school setting.

The Role of Universal Education

The phrase "universal education" ordinarily connotes education that is universally available. Citizens in a democracy have a right to education — indeed, an obligation to become "educated." It was Thomas Jefferson who wrote, "If a nation expects to be ignorant and free, in a state of civilization, it expects what never was and never will be." Thus universal education conjures up notions of equity, access, and equal opportunity. But the phrase also suggests education that is universal in the sense of being comprehensive, global, and multifaceted. Both connotations are important.

The role of universal education is to produce "viable" individuals. I use the term *viable* to mean individuals who are capable of sustaining an intellectual life, of growing and developing mentally. *Viable* shares roots with such words as *vivacious* and *vital*, which refer to potency, energy, and spirit. Viability derives from Dewey's idea: Education is life; life is education.

Free societies need individuals who can think for themselves and understand the perplexities of the modern world; who can direct their own behavior, respect the rights of others, and function effectively in an interdependent world.

The idea of viability is not original. It derives from scholars such as W.E.B. Du Bois (1868-1963) and George I. Sanchez (1906-1972). Du Bois, for example, was opposed to industrial education programs for African Americans because such programs served to limit individual education and life choices to narrowly conceived industrial crafts. The industrial education movement for blacks taught self-sufficiency, but only through servility. Such education trained African Americans (men principally) only to be good workers and followers. It did not expose them to the larger world of ideas or prepare them to be leaders. To Du Bois, industrial education prepared black males for inferiority (Du Bois 1903).

What Du Bois sought for blacks was education opportunities equal to those of whites in equitably funded, desegregated schools at a time when the *Plessy* v. *Ferguson* (1896) doctrine of "separate but equal" was in full force in many school systems. Du Bois, one of the founders of the National Association for the Advancement of Colored People (NAACP) along with people such as James Weldon Johnson and Moorfield Story, worked through the NAACP to lobby for court decisions supportive of integrated education that would provide equal education opportunities. He lived long enough to witness the landmark U.S. Supreme Court decision, *Brown* v. *Board of Education* (1954), which began the dismantling of school segregation in the United States.

George I. Sanchez devoted his life's work to the economic, political, and education problems of Mexican Americans in the Southwest, especially in Texas and New Mexico, where Hispanics had lived since the late 16th century. In spite of that long history, Hispanics were, to use Sanchez's word, "strangers" in their own land, a forgotten people (Sanchez 1940). Political corruption and greed deprived Mexican Americans of their land base and economic sustenance, making them second-class citizens. To Sanchez, education could be the only permanent solution to the problem. But, like Du Bois, he opposed education that was narrowly focused, such as community education experiments in New Mexico that aimed at providing Hispanic students with skills to be successful only in their own villages. Merely producing contented villagers was a poor goal in Sanchez's eyes. Instead, he sought the kind of education that would prepare Mexican-American students to explore — and to be successful — beyond their villages or, if they *chose* to remain in their villages, to transform them, bringing them into the modern world:

> He [the Mexican American] must learn to compete in his society more effectively, he must develop business acumen and learn economic values and he must be fitted to change his society both economically and culturally. (Sanchez 1940, p. 81)

Sanchez's critics argued that Mexican Americans could not benefit from such "emancipatory" education because they were inherently inferior to non-Hispanics and therefore incapable of self-determination. As proof, his critics cited Mexican-American students' low I.Q. scores. Sanchez showed that the I.Q. tests were culturally biased and, for many Spanish-speaking youngsters, virtually unintelligible (Parker 1972). Sanchez proposed bilingual-bicultural instruction in Spanish and English in the early grades to help Mexican-American students make the transition to an English-based curriculum. He believed that a bicultural curriculum would better prepare Mexican Americans to live in their own cultural community and in the larger, predominantly white community.

In the 1940s Sanchez worked with other Mexican Americans to revitalize a self-help association, the League of Latin American Citizens (LULAC). The association's goals were to promote equal education opportunities for Mexican Americans and to provide scholarships for college-bound students. He lived to see bilingual-bicultural education become a reality throughout much of the Southwest with the enactment of various state laws and with support from Title VII of the Elementary and Secondary Education Act of 1965 (Murillo 1996).

Although Du Bois and Sanchez dealt with very different cultural problems, the common theme of their work was to help educationally disenfranchised people to achieve "viability." They worked against prevailing tides of prejudice and indifference that trapped minority individuals in narrowly focused, inequitable schooling for subservience. Their goal was to achieve truly universal education — schooling that was culturally sensitive, that expanded rather than constricted the students' world, and schooling that was as accessible to minority individuals as it was to individuals in the dominant culture. Universal education is, by definition, emancipatory.

The examples of Du Bois and Sanchez focus on issues related to language, race, and culture, all of which are aspects of diversity. But diversity also includes other forms of "difference," such as religious beliefs, sex, and sexual orientation. Truly universal education, in both its connotations, must encompass all forms of diversity. It must be fully emancipatory. To amplify this point, I suggest that universal education must help students develop 1) autonomy as learners, 2) intellectual effectiveness, 3) cultural efficacy, and 4) a disposition for lifelong learning.

Autonomy as learners. In a free society individuals must set their own goals and direct their own behavior as learners. Emancipatory education frees the learner from externally imposed goals. Both Du Bois and Sanchez fought against education that predetermined students' futures, often along very narrow, servile paths. Both argued and worked for universal education that would allow students to determine their own futures by the goals they set for themselves and the vigor with which they worked toward those goals. Freedom requires that students become educational entrepreneurs.

Intellectual effectiveness. Universal education enables students to achieve intellectual competence in areas that are important to them as individuals and in areas that ensure them a rightful place in the larger society. Intellectual effectiveness means that individuals can function as productive members of society, not merely in the narrow confines of a smaller cultural community. Du Bois and Sanchez fought against education that made minority individuals into mere cogs. Universal education must engender a vision of the whole — a global vision, if you will — and provide the intellectual means for individuals to participate meaningfully in that vision.

Cultural efficacy. Modern transportation and communications continue to "shrink" our world, as the cliché goes. But, as is often the case, the cliché is accurate. Today, more than at any time in history, each person must recognize that he or she is a member of a global society. By definition, this global society is multicultural, highly diverse. Cultural efficacy, as a goal of universal (or emancipatory) education, means that individuals recognize the diversity of humanity and are capable of functioning effectively in the global culture, in addition to functioning within the closer confines of their home culture. Indeed, "home culture" itself may be variously defined for different purposes. In some cases the home culture may be a specific local community, a generalized cultural community (the "Hispanic community," the "gay community"), or a broader sense of "home" in the world, such as "American," "Canadian," or even "North American" or "Western."

Disposition for lifelong learning. Like the so-called shrinking of our world, modern technologies also have sped up the pace of change. The once idealized goal of becoming a lifelong learner is now a practical necessity. Therefore, universal education must engender in all students a "love of learning," if not for the sake of learning as a philosophically worthy pursuit, then certainly as a mechanism for self-preservation. Mortimer Adler, author of *The Paideia Proposal*, suggests:

> [As] we recognize that twelve years of general, nonspecialized schooling for all is the best policy — the most practical preparation for work — we should all realize that is not its sole justification. It is not only the most expedient kind of schooling, but it is also best . . . because it prepares our children to be good citizens and to lead good human lives. (1982, p. 20)

Viable individuals are those who can change and grow with the world around them. We live in dynamic times. Teachers must be intellectually dynamic, and they must help students to realize a similar dynamism in their own intellectual lives.

In suggesting these goals for universal education, I am aware that many other worthy goals exist. But these four accurately aim

13

at democratic ideals that are imbedded in education in and for a free society: autonomy, self-awareness, and adaptability, or a capacity for change and growth. How, then, should schools function to achieve these goals?

Schools as Communities

Schools reflect the communities from which they draw their students, teachers, and others involved in the education enterprise. These communities are not only the physical surroundings — the farms, the houses, the apartments, and other dwellings and the businesses that serve them — but also the affinity groups: the Asian-American community, the Hispanic community, the deaf community, the gay community, and so on. Diversity is imbedded in the very idea of community.

But schools also are communities in themselves. This factor is as important to recognize as are the external communities that contribute to and shape the nature of the school as a communal entity. Another way of expressing this notion is that schools are an extension of the family and, by extrapolation, are families themselves — just as communities are families by extension. This circular definition points up the fact that communities, families, and schools own many characteristics in common. Not least among these characteristics is that group viability (as school, as family, as community) is firmly tied to individual viability. In a free and democratic society, the school must rely — as the community must — on the civil interactions of its participants, who act out of respect for individuals who may be different from themselves and with whose opinions they may not always agree. Just as siblings may hold divergent viewpoints, so, too, may citizens disagree even on fundamental matters. However, just as effective families "stick together" in spite of differences, so, too, do communities and schools "stick together" by using the glue of civility and respect for diversity to achieve social unity.

Social unity — the hallmark of community — permits schools to achieve the universal education ends to which are owed the freedom of the nation and the individual freedoms that the nation's citizens may rightly claim. When the social unity of a school breaks down, when community dissolves into chaos or anarchy, then such a troubled school cannot succeed in fostering individual learning, much less universal education. Breakdowns of social unity most often arise from conflicts over diversity issues. Racial prejudice, denigration of a (non-English) native language, homophobia, and other attitudes of intolerance toward "differences" are root causes of social disunity. The incivility of intolerance disrupts learning; unchecked, it may destroy it.

As microcosms of the larger community (whether "larger" is taken to be local or global), schools also are a social preparation for adult community life. And so educators must ensure that schools are exemplars of effective community life in a democratic society. In the context of teaching for diversity, therefore, the building of effective community requires educators to form partnerships and to solve diversity problems.

Schools function best as exemplars of community when educators form partnerships with their constituents. Those constituents are not only students and their parents but also citizens (grandparents, business people) in the community who may have little direct contact with the schools. Often the reasons given for involving community citizens is that they are taxpayers and therefore have a financial stake in the schools' success and because the schools are training the future workers for the community's businesses and industries. But these are superficial reasons. A community's citizens have a stake in the success of the schools because, fundamentally, the schools are teaching the young people of the community how to become productive adult citizens.

This societal education, in turn, is one reason why a community's educators must solve diversity problems in the school. Diversity issues that arise in the microcosm of the school mirror such issues in the macrocosm of the community. Thus a societal education will be incomplete that does not include addressing diversity issues and solving problems rooted in diversity conflicts. In this regard teachers must be viewed as reformers and respected for their insights into the instructional processes that will facilitate such problem solving. Forming partnerships with parents and other community citizens may serve not only to assist in the solving of diversity problems but also to replicate in the community setting those solutions arrived at in the school — and vice versa.

In summary, in a free, democratic society individuals have the right to pursue their interests. The pursuit of self-interests, however, must be tempered by civility and respect for the rights of others to engage in similar pursuits. The U.S. Constitution and Bill of Rights, the Canadian Charter of Rights and Freedoms, and similar guiding documents in other democratic nations set down principles that speak to the need for balance between the rights of individuals and the rights of collectivities, such as the community or the nation. Such balance is constantly being negotiated. Civility is necessary for successful negotiation. Schools must be active participants in this societal dialogue, and educators must teach their students how to participate in the dialogue.

Universal education is thus an education for civil engagement that likewise balances the goal of helping students learn how to think for themselves with the goal of teaching students to understand and respect others who may be different from them in terms of culture, race, religious beliefs, sex, sexual orientation, and so on. Learner autonomy, intellectual effectiveness, cultural efficacy, and a disposition for lifelong learning are important touchstones for universal education that is aimed at developing "viable" individuals.

Finally, the schools must attend to both the micro- and macrocosmic impulses of community. They must be viable communities in themselves, but they also must be exemplars and teachers, assisting students to learn how best to become responsible citizens in a free society. To do so, educators must address diversity issues that often stand in the way of achieving community and must solve problems that arise from diversity-based disputes. Teaching for diversity requires not only that teachers understand and deal effectively with the differences before them in the classroom but also that they teach their students to understand and respect the diversity of individuals in the world around them, whether they are in school or out.

Chapter Two

IDENTIFYING AND UNDERSTANDING DIVERSITY ISSUES

Students pass through classrooms almost as passengers on a bus pass through the night, glimpsed only for a moment in lighted windows. In that fleeting passage teachers must learn their names, discover who they are and what they need, and, hopefully, teach them something of value. The more different that students are from their teachers, the more challenging is the task of knowing them and teaching them. How, then, can teachers hope to identify and understand the diversity issues that arise in the teaching of students from many backgrounds? Moreover, having made these necessary discoveries, how can teachers help their diverse students to face similar issues as they make their way in the world?

In attempting to answer these questions I would posit two essential attitudes for teachers. First, it is important for teachers to acknowledge — and work to understand — manifestations of "difference." Part of such acknowledgment must be a coming to terms with one's attitudes toward human differences. Second and equally important, teachers must recognize that human differences also extend to, even shape, learning styles and preferences.

Thus accommodating a variety of cognitive styles must be accepted as a basic challenge in effectively teaching for diversity.

Labels and Describing Diversity

It is all too easy to reduce to mere labels those who are different from us. "That student is *black*" often is used to say that the student "acts black," by which the labeler means that the student behaves in ways that are stereotypic of African Americans. "That student is *gay*" can mean that the student behaves in ways associated with homosexual stereotypes, such as flamboyant effeminacy. Such stereotypes ill-serve those they characterize. Therefore the problem with many labels is not just the label itself but also the connotations and stereotypes that the label conjures up.

Educators have developed the label "at risk," borrowing from medical jargon, to describe students who are in danger of failing in school and thus in need of special assistance. But, as well-meaning as this label is, it carries difficult baggage. "At risk" identifies a symptom. What really places a student at risk? That is, what gives rise to the symptom?

One school system in which I worked tried to pin down an answer by looking at the demographic question: Who is the at-risk student? We examined the demographics of secondary students who were academically struggling (making grades that averaged D or F). Common factors among this population turned out to be several: Most of the students were male, Hispanic, and from low-income families; most spoke English as their second language; and most had attended a certain elementary school. By looking at other students in the district who also were male, Hispanic, from a low-income background, and spoke English as a second language but were performing successfully in their academic classes, we were able to pinpoint a problem. These successful students came mostly from elementary schools that had bilingual education programs; the unsuccessful students tended to come from the one elementary school where this was not the case.

In this instance, therefore, the term "at risk" was defined, rather than used as a generic description or, worse, a stereotype. By defining the label, we were able to identify population characteristics and thus to identify a problem for which a solution could be developed.

To say that each student is unique, of course, is true; but it begs the question. In fact, many students are more alike than they are different. Where differences exist, realistic "labels" can provide a useful shorthand for discussion purposes. They can describe reasonable generalizations, for example. Students who are labeled "ADD" have in common certain characteristics associated with attention deficit disorder. Students who are labeled "LEP" have in common certain limitations in their understanding and use of English. But ADD students and LEP students differ from one another, often to a rather wide degree, within the label characteristics as well.

My point is simply this: Educators need to examine what lies behind a label and to recognize the limitations, as well as the utility, of labels that are applied to students.

Cultures as Frameworks for Understanding

The concept of culture is multifaceted, therefore some narrowing is essential for purposes of discussion. The aspect of culture that I will address in this section is principally that of the student, by which I mean his or her cultural background. This does not deny that students may have aspirations (or their parents may have aspirations for them) to attain the characteristics of a different culture. Nor does it disregard the cultures and subcultures of the school itself. But a student's cultural background is a useful framework for better understanding the individual student and, in many cases, groups of students from the same cultural background.

The first notion that must be dispensed with is the idea of high and low cultures. In the main, cultures are neither better nor worse than others; they are merely different from one another. An elitist notion of culture would hold, for example, that people who read Shakespeare and listen to classical music are high culture (therefore culturally better), whereas people who read supermarket tabloids and listen to rockabilly music are low culture (therefore culturally inferior). This is an essentially Western (Euro-American) conceit, but it often is perpetuated in the stereotyping of students. "White trash" and "trailer trash" — pejorative labels for impoverished white people — are stereotypic labels that are as much identified with so-called low culture attributes as with low socioeconomic status.

Students who are assigned low-status labels on the basis of cultural elitism often have a more difficult time in school because they not only must overcome such real limitations as poverty, but they also must overcome the stigma of assigned cultural inferiority. When a student so labeled has trouble learning, it is too easy to say, "Well, what would you expect? His family is just trailer trash." And so the victim of stereotyping is further victimized.

The problem of cultural elitism also extends into the curriculum, when teachers adopt a "heroes and holidays" approach to teaching about other cultures. Such an approach provides only token recognition of diversity, often delivered in ways that are, at best, patronizing. The dominant U.S. culture also is diminished by this approach, which reduces Revolutionary War-era history to Washington's Birthday — now lumped with Lincoln's as President's Day — and re-creations of the wounded fife-drum-and-flag trio in Independence Day parades.

While such diminished representations are almost worthless, even the best cultural awareness programs in schools have limitations. Culture is like an iceberg; most of it lies below the surface. It is submerged in the subconscious, woven into the very fabric of family and community life. At that subconscious level it determines the behaviors and attitudes that are defined as good or bad, acceptable or unacceptable, worthy or unworthy. These values are manifest in and reinforced by the rituals, folkways, and other behaviors that are the visible part of the iceberg. Thus we can teach *about* a culture and we can help those outside the culture to participate in cultural rituals, but we cannot teach people a culture at the subconscious level. This is an important understanding.

It is important to realize that the converse also is true: A person's inherent culture cannot be eliminated, because it is deeply embedded in the individual's subconscious.

Thus the real issue in teaching about cultures becomes one of attaining balance. Effective teachers help students to negotiate cultural attributes so that they can develop their own identities. A student's home culture is developed through socialization in the home and community. Nurturing parents convey cultural attitudes to their children without conscious intent, starting with how they hold and talk to their infants. For example, as the father of twins, a boy and a girl, I found myself rough-housing more with my son than with his twin sister. In this way, I realized later, I acted out stereotypes: "Boys are strong" and "girls are fragile." These traditional gender stereotypes undoubtedly were passed on to me by my parents, and I conveyed them to my children.

Traditional male-female role stereotypes (machismo versus delicacy, for example) are part of my Spanish-Mexican cultural heritage. But such machismo also is a stereotype, because the same character traits that define Hispanic machismo are present in other cultures.

Schools affect a student's development of self-identity, sometimes intentionally and sometimes unintentionally. For example, the school curriculum is intentional. What is studied conveys cultural attitudes. Studying famous men — Washington, Lincoln, Kennedy — may help to define what the school culture considers to be "good." Studying classic literature — Shakespeare, Milton — can do the same. These examples might point to a "high culture," elitist curriculum orientation or, depending on how famous men and classic literature are juxtaposed with other curricular choices, might simply be part of a balanced approach to culture.

At the same time teachers, administrators, counselors, and others in the school setting also convey cultural attitudes without conscious intent. How teachers interact with one another in the presence of students, how they interact with students, and how they encourage students to interact with one another are forms of socialization by which culture is negotiated. Taken together, both the intentional and unintentional affect students' development of self-identity and the development of the school culture itself, which I alluded to at the start of this chapter. Thus the total school culture, as well as the individuals within that culture, affect the individual and modify the socialization of the home and the community.

To whom (or to what) does a student owe cultural allegiance? The answer is existential and situational. As Cushner, McClelland, and Safford suggest:

> All people sometimes act according to their individual interests, and sometimes according to their group allegiance. The relative emphasis on group versus individual orientation varies from group to group and may affect significantly the choices one makes. (1992, p. 92)

Students, as all people do, possess no single culture. Rather, their self-identity is composed of many cultures. Thus how they choose to learn and to behave may be based on the cultural attributes of their home, of the school, of their peer group, or some combination of these influences. Such complexity is essential in the creation of the individual. And the recognition of such complexity also is essential for sensitive, individualistic teaching. While it may be tempting to attribute a student's behavior to a cultural stereotype — "What do you expect? She's Hmong!" — the simplistic label is as useless in the education of the student as it is demeaning to the student while showing ignorance of the student's cultural background.

In the next several sections of this chapter, I will deal with characteristics that influence students' cultural self-identity and how educators identify and understand diversity issues. These characteristics include language development, socioeconomic status, stigma and resistance, learning style preferences, gender identity and sexual orientation, race and ethnicity, and religion.

Language Development

Learning to talk is as natural as learning to walk. People have a built-in capacity for learning, processing, and creating language. They are equally capable of learning more than one language, though in the United States and, to a lesser extent, in Canada there has existed a belief that native bilingualism is abnormal (Fishman 1966). All children acquire language as a part of natural maturation, going through phases of listening, babbling, telegraphic speech ("me hungry"), and utterances of irregular syntax patterns ("Daddy threw mother from the train a kiss").

By the age of five or six, most children speak their native language with conventional syntax and using all of the sounds of that language. They know how to use the basic phonetic, syntactic, and grammar rules of the language. What they have yet to learn are all of the idiosyncrasies of the language, its nuances and idiomatic expressions.

But language is only one building block of what is called "communicative competence," which includes gesture, visual and vocal expressiveness, and such language-driven elements as speech, reading, and writing. Communicative competence, which begins to be acquired naturally at birth, is aided by language instruction at school. Thus such language instruction must encompass the full range of communicative competence, not merely traditional reading and writing. This is particularly true for students learning a second language — and thus a second cultural context.

Communicative competence is not necessarily culture-bound — some communication *is* universal, or nearly so — but it does develop and take place within a cultural context. And some elements may be culture-bound. For example, simple gestures, such as the hand-waggling gesture that denotes "come here" among American youngsters, are not universal. The waggling *hand-up* "come here" gesture typically seen in the United States and Canada is "translated" as a *hand-down* waggling in certain Asian cultures.

About two-thirds of any message (meaning) exchanged in face-to-face communication is accomplished through gestures, facial expressions, and vocal intonations, not words alone. In fact, words may be entirely absent. A mother's smile can be sufficient encouragement for a child to persevere in a difficult task; a mother's frown can discourage misbehavior.

Formal language learning in school, therefore, must include more than reading and writing if the aim is to help students who are learning a second language to become more than merely literate — to become communicatively competent and thus able to convey meaning through nonliterate forms.

At the same time, such formal language learning also must enable students to achieve "academic competence," which is the ability to use language for higher-order thinking — to make and understand abstractions and metaphors, for example — without resort to social cues. Communicative competence is socially functional language (in the roundest sense of the word *language*). Academic competence is required for the construction of meaning from texts and for interacting with ideas.

When teachers work with second-language learners, they must learn to distinguish communicative competence from academic competence. For example, students may be highly competent in using English at the communicative level without being competent to any degree in using English at the academic level. One difficulty that arises in integrating new learners of English into English-only academic classes is that they often give evidence of communicative competence, and teachers mistakenly assume that communicative competence to mean that the students will be able to function successfully in the academic setting. Teachers should not be surprised to find that such students may not have much success because their communicative competence is not yet matched by academic competence in the target language.

The purpose of bilingual education programs in the United States and Canada is to help students achieve both communicative and academic competence, ideally so that they can function successfully in both their native language and their second language. Typically, bilingual education maintains the student's academic achievement by teaching academic subject matter in the student's native language, while simultaneously helping the student to acquire communicative and academic competence in the second, or target, language.

Critics of bilingual education often claim that a student's academic achievement likely will suffer, because the academic subject matter is taught only in the first language. However, this is not the case. Both U.S. and Canadian researchers have reported no decline of academic achievement (Lambert and Tucker 1972; Macnamara 1972; Cummins 1988; Garcia 1983). On the contrary, such researchers consistently report that bilingual education tends to increase scholastic achievement when academic competence is approached through teaching in the student's first language.

Socioeconomic Status

For both monolingual and bilingual students, socioeconomic status can play a hand in early language competence (Cazden 1988; Rice 1989). While language acquisition is natural to all youngsters, poverty and its social ramifications can affect the development of both communicative and academic competence, but especially the latter. Human development specialists Hart and Risley (1995) conducted a 2½-year longitudinal study, observing 42 families for an hour each month while the parents conversed with their children as the children were learning to talk. The families were from two types of homes, characterized as "professional" (university professors' families) and "poverty" (welfare families). Hart and Risley concluded that:

> the most important difference among families was the amount of talking that went on. . . . increased amounts of talking provided some children vastly more experience with nearly every quality feature of language and interaction. (p. 192)

Not only did professors' homes include more talk, but the talk also was of a higher quality. Hart and Risley identified these quality features:

- Language diversity. More talk in professional homes also meant a broader use of language than in poverty homes.
- Feedback tone. Professional homes provided more encouragement (positive tone), whereas poverty homes offered discouragement (negative tone).
- Symbolic emphasis. Professional homes offered stronger emphasis on relationships between words (names) and events.
- Guidance style. Professional homes tended to emphasize "asking," while poverty homes tended to emphasize "demanding."
- Responsiveness style. Professional homes sought to control behavior by rewarding good behavior; poverty homes controlled behavior by punishing bad behavior.

Parents in professional homes engaged their children more often in dialogue; therefore, not only was there more language, there also was more interaction through the use of language. Hart and Risley's findings on parental interaction also echo earlier studies in England (Bernstein 1970) and the United States (Maccoby and Martin 1983).

Studies such as these point to the need for early education to overcome the limiting effects of poverty on language development. Head Start and similar programs provide such early education on the premise that supplementing impoverished students' home language experiences will help such children to be able to succeed in academic learning on par with their more advantaged peers.

Detrimental effects on language learning, however, are not the only school problems associated with poverty. The "poverty line" in the United States currently is about $15,000 annual income for a family of four, but few would argue that poverty relates only to income. Perhaps more important are the effects of poverty on beliefs, attitudes, and expectations.

Individuals living in poverty often believe (not without justification) that they are not in control of their lives — indeed, that controlling their lives is beyond their power or ability. Impoverished persons often express fatalistic attitudes — "failure is inevitable when you're poor" — and accompany such attitudes with despondency — "things will never get better." And so individuals living in poverty often have low expectations for themselves and for their children — "if failure is inevitable, why try?"

Teachers who accept these beliefs and attitudes enable children from poverty homes to fulfill their lowest expectations. However, educators who refuse to accept such self-defeating beliefs and attitudes can make a difference for the better in the lives of such children and, in turn, for their families. The choice of these two stances is between what I call the "equalizer" and the "allocator." Schools and individual educators who buy into the self-defeating beliefs of the "culture of poverty" — there are universals among persons in poverty — become role "allocators." They assign students, not necessarily directly but by the ways in which they teach them, to certain life roles. Often they channel impoverished students into the education conduits that lead only to low-status, low-pay employment. At the same time, they channel students from high-socioeconomic-status families into the education conduits that lead to professional, high-status, high-pay careers.

"Equalizers," on the other hand, are educators who help all children, regardless of socioeconomic status, to fulfill their potential to the best of their ability. These are the educators who work to achieve, to the best of *their* ability, the grand design of U.S. and Canadian public education — that is, education that can lift up those in poverty. Education, promise-laden when viewed in this philosophy (as much political as educational), is to be the Great Equalizer. But that promise has yet to be fully realized.

Allocating roles to students on the basis of socioeconomic factors sustains social class stratification and perpetuates (and is perpetuated by) curricular emphasis on high-culture versus low-culture subject matter. Stereotypic labeling also helps to maintain the status quo. Two decades ago U.S. education critics depicted schools as sorting machines whose main purpose, though never stated as such, was to mirror and maintain social stratification (Spring 1989; Katz 1976; Bowles and Gintis 1976). They — as have critics since then — regarded such instructional strategies as ability grouping (academic tracking) as mechanisms for preserving the status quo. By tracking students, ostensibly for academic purposes, schools could reasonably ensure that low-socioeconomic students would end up in low-status, low-pay occupations, while high-socioeconomic students, being tracked in the high-culture lane (college-bound), would end up in high-status, high-pay careers.

The stratification in schools was aptly described in the 1980s by John Goodlad. His 10-year study of 1,016 classrooms, 1,350 teachers, and 17,163 students — reported in *A Place Called School* (1984) — yielded, among other results, the conclusion that most schools operated a two-track system. One track was college-preparatory, the other utilitarian. The college-prep track was high-culture; the utilitarian track was low-culture, or in Goodlad's terms:

> High track classes devoted more time to relatively high level cognitive processes — making judgments, drawing inferences. . . . Low track classes devoted time to rote learning and application of knowledge and skills. (p. 131)

Advocates of academic tracking claim that placement is based solely on intellectual ability. However, a number of researchers — for example, Oakes (1985) and Anyon (1989) — have shown a high correspondence between students' social class and their placement in a given track, beginning as early as the fifth grade. This is not surprising, given what we know about the effects of poverty on language and academic development.

Canada faces a similar problem. There, tracking (or "streaming") also begins in the elementary grades, as it does in the United States. Sium (1989), studying one of Canada's largest metropolitan school systems, reported that the low-academic (basic) tracks in its secondary schools contained a disproportionate number of students whose parents were recent, working-class immigrants from Jamaica, Punjabi, Vietnam, Greece, and various Latin American nations.

Things did not improve when students reached the middle years. During the seventh and eighth grades, students were allowed to select among the various utilitarian (job preparation) or college preparatory streams. Aided by the advice of teachers, counselors, or principals — and influenced by the fact that they were grouped by ability in the elementary grades and possessed little vision about where each stream ran — most of the immigrant students selected a utilitarian stream. Once in this "basic" stream, they were not allowed to change to a higher level.

Many students eventually came to regret their choice. One student described the situation he and his classmates found themselves in:

> By the time they get to Grade 11 and they know what is happening to them, it is already too late. They are used to doing nothing, and they came to love it. (Sium 1989, p. 175)

None of the students interviewed for Sium's study liked being in the basic stream; they did not realize what they were getting into when they made the choice. Four of the students (out of 32 interviewed) actually changed schools, or school systems, in order to get into a higher stream. Although Sium cautions against making generalizations from this ethnographic study, he nonetheless suggests that the situation in this metropolitan school district may be symptomatic of the type of education offered to Canadian working-class students.

Stigma and Resistance

Before leaving the characteristic of socioeconomic status entirely, it seems pertinent to discuss more specifically the stigma of poverty and resistance culture. In the previous section I dealt with the school's (and individual educators') reactions to students from poor families. But what provokes such reactions? Often the reactions arise from deeper wells than merely a shallow desire (whether conscious or subconscious) to maintain the status quo of social stratification.

31

The stigma of poverty is a social interaction factor that operates between members of an out-group (the "have nots") and an in-group (the "haves"). The "haves" tend to treat the "have nots" as inferior to themselves. Such factors as less money, less up-to-date apparel, and less elegant language equate to less "humanness." Thus the stigma of poverty is one of lesser humanity in the eyes of those who are not poor. Because they are "haves," teachers of poor children often believe (or behave from a subconscious belief) that such children are inferior — less capable of learning, less willing to learn — in short, less human than children who are more advantaged (Kozol 1991). The power of stigmatization is that what teachers believe and translate into expectations for poor children is what poor children come to believe about themselves. Teachers who expect children to fail create children who fail.

The psychology of poverty is a psychology of suppression. The stigma of poverty produces a self-fulfilling prophecy when students live *down* to their teachers' (and parents') low expectations for them. This is not new information, of course. More than 20 years ago Rosenthal and Rubin (1976) reviewed 345 experiments that tested the efficacy of this self-fulfilling prophecy and concluded that the "reality of the phenomenon is beyond doubt. . . . the effects of interpersonal expectations were as great, on the average, in everyday life situations as they were in laboratory experiences" (p. 414). A few years later Good (1981) conducted a meta-analysis of 18 studies dealing with teacher expectations and the self-fulfilling prophecy and concluded that teachers are unaware, for the most part, that they "vary their behavior toward high- and low-achieving students" to the detriment of the low-achieving students. Good observed several ways that teachers varied their behavior toward high- and low-achievers. Examples include:

- Teachers tended to communicate less with low-achievers and to call on them less often.
- Teachers made eye contact less often with low-achievers they did call on and gave low-achievers less time to respond to questions.

- Teachers praised low-achievers less than they praised high-achievers when they risked answering questions about which they were unsure.
- Teachers criticized low-achievers more than high-achievers for making inaccurate responses to questions.
- Teachers tended to provide fewer details and less precise feedback to low-achievers.
- Teachers demanded less homework and less effort from low-achievers.

Thus poor children who also are low-achievers tend to remain low-achievers not merely because the conditions of poverty suppress their ability to achieve but, in addition, because their teachers unwittingly act as suppressors of ability. The negative effects of the self-fulfilling prophecy on low-income students is compounded when the students are from minority groups, as Canadian and U.S. studies have shown (Cummins 1988; U.S. Commission on Civil Rights 1973).

However, a reactive psychology counteracts the psychology of suppression. When teachers are suppressors of ability, it is a small step across a thin line in the minds of students to see teachers as *oppressors*. From that perception arises an attitude of resistance. This attitude, viewed in group terms, is called "resistance culture."

When students from a poverty background resist the efforts of educators to teach them — particularly when "teaching" is viewed as changing them to fit the mold of the dominant culture, the elite culture — then such resistance is a cultural defense strategy. By resisting what the school has to offer, low-income students retain their social-class identity.

Resistance culture is an interesting phenomenon. A study done in England by Paul Willis (1977) reported resistance-culture behavior by lower-class English youngsters. These "lads," a name they called themselves, perceived high grades, speaking the "Queen's English," and cooperating with the teachers as a threat to their group identity. In the United States, Ogbu (1986) reported similar resistance-culture behavior among low-income African-

American students. Resistance culture turns dominant-culture values upside down. In the dominant culture, reading well is high-status; in the resisting culture, therefore, reading well becomes low-status. Thus failure becomes a cultural badge of honor.

Resistance culture is reinforced by the stereotyping of low-income children as less intelligent, less capable, and less willing than their more advantaged peers. It also is perpetuated when schools reduce minority-culture attributes to second-class status, such as in a "heroes and holidays" curriculum that trivializes non-dominant cultures. To overcome resistance culture, students (and their parents) must see the promise of education as applicable to them, not just to their more advantaged peers — indeed, they must see their more advantaged age mates truly as *peers*, not as members of a class apart.

Learning Style Preferences

One of my ninth-grade students once asked me: "How can I find out how intelligent I am?" I was taken aback by the question. He was a precocious student and the answer seemed to be self-evident. I asked him whether it would make a difference in how he felt about himself if he knew. His answer was curious: "Well, not if I'm shown to be highly intelligent! But what if I'm shown to be dumb? I'd feel like heck." I decided to survey all of my students by asking them to define what human intelligence meant to them.

The students defined intelligence in a couple of ways: Human intelligence is the total knowledge an individual acquires, and intelligence also refers to the ability of humans to acquire knowledge and then to adapt to new conditions and situations by using that knowledge. Their definitions conformed to those of most psychologists. And they seemed like pretty intelligent answers to me.

Would they really like to know whether they were intelligent or how intelligent they were? Perhaps — or perhaps not. "I'd rather not know," one student explained. "That way, if I'm dumb, I won't know it."

Early in the 20th century a central debate in education was whether intelligence was a general aptitude or the composite of many singular aptitudes. Intelligence then — and only slightly less so now, at least in the popular mind — was tied to knowledge of the dominant culture. Thus it was argued that African Americans, Hispanics, and Native Americans, for example, were less intelligent because they were less knowledgeable in terms of the dominant culture. Even today there are great problems in the testing industry with regard to ensuring that standardized tests are "culture-fair." Some critics wonder if it is possible to construct any single test so that it is truly culture-fair. But that is only one problem with a focus on general aptitude intelligence testing.

Stephen Jay Gould, in *The Mismeasure of Man* (1981), demonstrated some of the other vagaries of intelligence testing. For example, he showed that there is greater variance of scores within racial groups than between racial minorities and whites in I.Q. tests. And Gould raised the question, as other researchers have, of relying on any single test (or battery of tests) to "measure" intelligence.

A useful definition of intelligence that is fully in line with the one posed by my ninth-graders is that intelligence consists of "multiple capabilities" that manifest as the ability to create products, to learn from experience, and to solve problems (Snyderman and Rothman 1987). Howard Gardner, the Harvard psychologist, developed his "multiple intelligences" theory along these lines. Originally, he posited seven "intelligences": logical-mathematical, linguistic, musical, spatial, bodily-kinesthetic, interpersonal, and intrapersonal (Gardner and Hatch 1989). More recently, Gardner added a naturalist intelligence.

Gardner's notions of intelligence have been taken up by a number of other psychologists and educators — for example, Slavin (1994) and Woolfolk (1995) — because of their utility in describing the differing abilities of individuals. "Intelligence" is no longer thought of as static. Rather, a student's intelligences — plural — are dynamic and related to time, place, subject matter, and other factors.

Viewing intelligence as dynamic, rather than static, means that teachers can identify specific student strengths and then use those strengths to extend learning in areas where the student is having difficulty. Thus in acting on the theory of multiple intelligences, teachers also reify constructivist learning theory, which posits that individuals "construct" knowledge by integrating new information into existing understandings. Such construction takes place in the dynamic contexts of various forms of intelligence, or "intelligences," to use Gardner's term.

Multiple intelligences and constructivist teaching theories are complemented by learning styles theory, which suggests that individuals learn in many different ways. Therefore, truly effective teaching and learning must take all of these ways into consideration. Some students learn best by quietly reading, others by actively doing. In the 1980s much attention was paid to learning styles theory as a way of identifying how students learn best. The idea was that, having identified a student's favored learning style(s), the teacher then could tailor instruction so that the student could learn most effectively.

Unfortunately, the use of elaborate "learning style inventories" became, in some schools and school districts at least, another way to label *groups* of students. For example, Hispanic students might be lumped together as "field dependent learners" according to a learning style inventory, with the result that all Hispanic students were treated alike. Not surprisingly, this strategy failed. Of course, not all Hispanic students learn the same way. The point of attempting to determine how students learn best is to match teaching to *individual* learning styles. However, this misuse did raise a pertinent question: What about culture? Could at least some learning style preferences be culture-bound?

Culture is one of the "other factors" that I alluded to a couple of paragraphs ago. I can sketch a response to this question by relating a story. When I taught about demonstration speeches in the public school setting, I usually spent only a little time describing how to give a demonstration speech. I would give a brief example, such as demonstrating how to hold a golf club and swing it. Then I would ask for volunteers to give an impromptu demonstration speech. After a moment or two of initial shyness, invariably several volunteers would step forward. But this lesson went differently when I tried it with Native American students going to school on the Crow Reservation in Montana.

I thought I had established a good rapport with the Crow students; but when I asked for volunteers to give the impromptu demonstration speech, I was disappointed that no one volunteered. At first I took this to indicate that I had done something wrong. Had I somehow communicated that the impromptu demonstration speech would be too risky? I was puzzled. Then, about a week later, five of the 10 students in the class volunteered to give a demonstration speech — and they all did very well. What had happened?

As I reflected on this incident, it occurred to me that the Crow students were following the traditional pattern of learning and communicating that reflected their culture. Most Western school culture communicates that it is okay to risk looking silly in an impromptu demonstration speech. This is a low-risk activity when undertaken before a teacher who gives every appearance of being trustworthy. On the other hand, traditional Crow culture emphasizes thorough observation of a task to be performed and practice for mastery before a "public" performance, such as a demonstration speech in class. Impromptu performance is devalued. My Crow students were learning and communicating from the basis of a cultural tradition with which I was unfamiliar.

The work of Susan Phillips (1983) with Native Americans and Geneva Gay (1974, 1991) with African-American students yielded similar results. Teachers often misinterpret their students' behaviors because they do not understand the students' learning and communication styles. Such styles differ not only among individuals but also according to cultural traditions that are transmitted to children at home and within the cultural community.

I have gathered a number of ideas together in this section on learning style preferences in order to establish another part of the foundation for identifying and understanding diversity issues. I will wait until Chapter Three to explore how educators can use such identification and understanding to shape instruction to accommodate diversity of all sorts.

Gender Identity and Sexual Orientation

Gender identity and sexual orientation are additional factors in identifying and understanding diversity. They are related but certainly not the same, though both seemingly are driven by biology and culture. Researchers may argue the extent to which gender identity is influenced by the individual's sex (biology) or environment (culture), but the conclusion most scientists make is that both forces are involved. The same is true for sexual orientation. Furthermore, both gender identity and sexual orientation become apparent at various ages. The most that can be said is that gender identity tends to show itself earlier, usually sometime in elementary school, while sexual orientation becomes more certain later, usually during middle school or high school, sometimes in adulthood.

A quarter-century ago Maccoby and Jacklin (1974) reviewed the school records of more than 1,500 elementary school pupils and reported that girls and boys differed significantly in several behaviors. Girls performed equally well compared to boys in mathematics and visual-spatial activities during the first three years of elementary school, for example. By sixth grade, however, girls were less aggressive than boys, girls performed verbally better than boys, and boys performed better in mathematics and visual-spatial activities. These behavioral differences have been attributed both to basic genetic differences between the sexes and to differentiated socialization practices, with the weight of the scholarship leaning heavily toward sex-differentiated socialization practices as the explanation for gender differences in school performance. But the biological basis of gender differences should not be discounted. Genetic differences may explain differences in academic and social behavior in school, at least to some extent. Sociobiologist Edward O. Wilson, in his book, *On Human Nature* (1978), suggests that:

> modest genetic differences exist between the sexes; the behavioral genes interact with virtually all existing environments to create noticeable divergence in early psychological development; and the divergence is almost always widened

38

in later psychological development by cultural sanctions and training. (p. 133)

Gender identity has to do with an individual's identification with socially assigned roles. Western cultural norms set certain expectations for men and different expectations for women. For much of history women were seen as subservient to men, and that legacy is still very much alive. After all, women's suffrage in the United States became a reality less than a century ago. And in spite of the women's rights movement that captured national attention in the 1970s, even today women and men are treated differently under the law in many areas of life.

In school, girls who adopt a male gender identity and boys who adopt a female gender identity become frequent targets of ridicule or abuse. "Tomboys" and "sissies" are contrary gender identities. In the past many teachers responded to such students by exhorting them to "act like a girl" or "act like a boy" — in other words, urging the students to adopt the stereotypic gender roles. An alternative approach might be to teach the broader value of diversity, which asserts every individual's right to behave as an individual, without regard for role stereotypes.

Sexual orientation, in contrast to gender identity, has to do with an individual's sexual interest in members of the same or opposite sex, or both sexes. While gender identity is largely produced by socialization and therefore manifests at an early age, sexual orientation manifests about the time of puberty or thereafter, when sexual interest awakens. Same-sex orientation (homosexuality) often is confused with gender identity because of stereotypical representations. Gay males can be seen as having a female gender identity if they exhibit effeminate behaviors; lesbians can be seen as having a male gender identity if they exhibit masculine behaviors. But, in fact, gender identity and sexual orientation are quite different concepts, and many gay males and lesbians do not exhibit alternative gender identities. Except for matters of sexual affinity, they are indistinguishable from heterosexual males and females.

While social prejudice against homosexuality is deeply embedded in Western history, cultural norms have varied from century to century. Homosexuality has been regarded as more normal in some periods, more perverse in others. Although the pendulum is swinging toward greater tolerance and acceptance of homosexuality today, prejudice against homosexuals persists. More than a quarter-century ago the American Psychiatric Association reclassified homosexuality, removing it from the category of mental disorders and stating that it was, instead, simply a lifestyle. Thus in examining issues of diversity, it should be recognized that:

> homosexuality is a normal variation in both sexual orientation and sexual behavior. Negative attitudes toward homosexuals are primarily the result of homophobia, a prejudice similar in nature and dynamics to all other prejudices. (Harbeck 1991, p. 12)

Indeed, students (usually in middle school or high school, more often the latter) who self-identify as gay or lesbian are likely to face many problems that arise from prejudice against homosexuals. And homophobia also can result in abuse directed toward heterosexual young people who behave in ways that are stereotypically gay or lesbian. Homophobic harassment also is frequently directed at the children of homosexuals, even though the children themselves may be heterosexual:

> One cannot overstate the devastating psychological effect . . . on the children of lesbians and gay men. The children of gays and lesbians may be harassed at school; teachers and other adult authorities might even be unwilling to come to their defense. (Blumfeld 1992, p. 117)

For youth who do identify themselves as gay or lesbian, the burden of homophobia may be very heavy. According to Hetrick and Martin:

> Most gay and lesbian teens pass through a turbulent and isolated period that brings the risk of developing maladaptive behaviors, and feelings of alienation, anxiety, depression, self-hatred, and demoralization. (1987, p. 28)

Adolescents who identify as homosexual (even if only to themselves) adopt a highly stigmatized role. While demographers may argue about the size of the homosexual population (variations often are based on how "homosexual" is defined), the Kinsey figure of 10% is used most often as a "rule of thumb" (Whitlock 1989). This is an enormous number of students across the United States and Canada — students who are demonstrably at higher risk than heterosexual students for substance abuse and suicide (Bell and Weinberg 1981; Uribe 1989). In fact, researchers have estimated that about one-third of homosexual youth have attempted suicide, and about one-third of all teen suicides are completed by gay and lesbian youth (Flax 1990).

Schools and classrooms are lonely and often violent places for homosexual teens. DeStefano (1988) reported a high incidence of physical attacks against gay and lesbian students. However, after such attacks, it often was the homosexual youngster who was referred for disciplinary action — even though he or she did nothing to provoke an attack.

Homophobia is so deeply ingrained in both community and school cultures that teachers and counselors often report fear of being ridiculed or harassed if they are seen to be supportive of homosexual teens. Many schools, either informally or by policy, discourage teacher support of gay youth or discussion of gay topics. Blatant homophobia also prevents many gay teachers and counselors from revealing their sexual orientation. Thus highly professional, highly respected educators who might serve as positive role models for young people struggling with sexual orientation issues are prevented from doing so for fear of job loss through legal or extra-legal means.

Gender identity is a factor of diversity, and the rules are in flux. Not long ago this struck me head-on when I walked into an airport men's room to find a young father changing his infant's diapers. His wife was outside at a pay telephone sending a fax to her office. But what seems like role reversal in this situation is merely a renegotiation of gender identity. Such renegotiation happens in the macrocosm of Western society just as it happens in the microcosm of individual families, where two working adults must negotiate (and juggle) the once tradition-bound roles of homemaker and breadwinner.

Sexual orientation is a factor of diversity no less than gender identity. Huge numbers of students are affected. As much as 10% of the student population may be gay or lesbian; many more students struggle with the issues before they figure out their sexual orientation. Moreover, experts suggest that between 8 million and 14 million children are being reared in gay and lesbian homes. These youngsters also are affected by homophobia and other sexual orientation issues.

Race and Ethnicity

Race and ethnicity are factors of diversity in several ways. They are tied to culture, language development, and socioeconomic status. They can influence gender identity and affect responses to sexual orientation issues. These are all crossing points for types of diversity. For schools, perhaps the most visible crossing points are those having to do with intellectual development and academic achievement.

The National Assessment of Educational Progress (NAEP) reports on achievement in the core academic subjects: reading, writing, mathematics, science, and social studies. On the NAEP assessments, white, non-Hispanic students consistently outperform African-American and Hispanic students (Byrnes 1996). This is not untypical. In fact, in many schools and districts these results are replicated in local and state tests of academic achievement as indicated by students' grades in school. And the NAEP assessments, which are a rather recent development, reiterate a longstanding observation that most minority students do not perform as well on academic tasks as majority white students. Why? It is a simple question, of course. But the answers are far from simple. They can be clustered into three categories of interpretation: cognitive and environmental deficit, unequal access to knowledge, and cultural incompatibility.

Cognitive and environmental deficit. This interpretation is two-pronged. Some researchers and theorists argue that Hispanic and African-American students are "hardwired" with less intellectual ability than white, non-Hispanic students (Herrnstein and Murray 1994; Jensen 1969). Because Hispanic and African-American students possess less capability for intelligence, the cognitive-deficit proponents reason, it is futile to expect such students to achieve beyond that limited intellectual capacity — in other words, it is futile to expect them to perform as well as white, non-Hispanic students. This reasoning has educational and socioeconomic consequences.

If African-American and Hispanic students are "programmed" for lower-level intellectual achievement, then academic intervention programs are of little use. Therefore, the cognitive-deficit proponents suggest, it would be in the "best interests" of Hispanic and African-American students if schools were to prepare them for the trades (rather than the professions), for which they are intellectually better suited. This line of reasoning, of course, is precisely what W.E.B. Du Bois and George Sanchez vigorously opposed. More recently, James A. Banks has been a leading voice in this opposition.

The second prong of the deficit interpretation is the argument that most Hispanic and African-American students are not themselves cognitively defective, but they live in "defective" environments, which either produce or compound their cognitive deficits compared to white, non-Hispanic students. Environmental-deficit proponents suggest that interventions directed at the Hispanic and African-American students' environments could be productive. Suggested interventions include improving living standards — specifically the diets and general health of pregnant women — and lifestyles, such as combating the disintegration of the traditional family and the proliferation of single-parent and teenage-parent families.

Early education for children, in contrast to the cognitive-deficit proponents' view, is seen as potentially efficacious. Environmental-deficit proponents argue strongly that poverty causes the majority of problems that Hispanics and African Americans experience in schools, because poverty causes students to live in "defective" environments. Therefore, by combating the effects of poverty, society can raise the intellectual capabilities and academic achievement of Hispanics and African Americans, who then can freely choose whatever life and career paths they want.

Unequal access to knowledge. This interpretation is perhaps the predominant one. It posits that Hispanic and African-American students do less well in academic work than do white, non-Hispanic students because they also have less access to education (Diaz 1992). Both the quality and the quantity of education available to most Hispanic and African-American students, this socioeconomic argument goes, is lower than that available to white, non-Hispanic students. Critiques of schooling and schools by Anyon (1989), Goodlad (1984), Oakes (1985), and others bolster this interpretation.

This interpretation is longstanding, coming to the fore in the 1950s. It formed the basis for arguments against segregated schooling. In the famous 1954 U.S. Supreme Court decision, *Brown* v. *Board of Education,* the Court reasoned that "separate but equal" schools could not exist and that, in fact, racially separate schools deprived minority children of equal education opportunities *even though the physical facilities and other tangible factors might be equal.* In reality the schools attended by minority children, almost always mostly poor children, were not equal to the schools attended by majority white children in the 1950s in terms of physical facilities or other factors. Many schools even today, social and education critics contend (and almost no one would deny), are unequal: Schools whose students are drawn from poor neighborhoods are almost invariably of poorer quality than those whose students come from middle-class and upper-class neighborhoods.

Cultural incompatibility. The third interpretation is, in some respects, a cultural extension of the second. This interpretation posits that minority students cannot benefit equally compared to majority students in schools where minority students experience "cultural incongruity." In other words, in schools where the school culture of the majority is significantly different from — and "locks out" — the minority culture, minority students are hampered if they cannot make a smooth transition from their home culture to the school culture (Reyhner 1992).

Equal education opportunity, the cultural incompatibility argument goes, cannot be achieved because the cultural mismatch interferes with the transmission of knowledge. For example, when the communication styles of teachers and students conflict, there is a breakdown in communication. Gay surmised that:

> the problems that culturally different students have with achieving success in school may be more procedural than intellectual. They may have the knowledge, or the capability to learn, but they may not know how to transmit it through the methods used in school. (1994, p. 82)

If the contents of the curriculum and the methods of instruction fail to recognize, value, and incorporate the minority culture, then minority students are bound to do less well compared to majority students whose home culture matches the school culture. Thus is laid a foundation for multicultural education — education for diversity — which is aimed at resolving cultural incompatibility.

I should say at this point, however, that the foundation for multicultural education has been laid in any case by the second argument as well. Sensitivity to diverse learners, regardless of the nature of that diversity, will assist educators in creating equal education — for students who come from various language backgrounds, for students of different races, for students from different cultures, and so on.

The weakest of the three interpretations, in my view and in the view of most educators, is the first. Few serious scholars are willing to argue that the brains of individuals from different races are essentially different from one another. This argument smacks of racial elitism, which scientific research readily debunks.

Religion

Religious differences also are factors of diversity, and how educators respond to those differences affects how students and their parents understand and feel about the school experience. In some cases culture and religion intertwine, which may complicate matters; and the connection of culture and religion also can give rise to stereotypes, which may be detrimental to communication and education.

A couple of illustrations come to mind. The first is drawn from personal experience. Once, when my children were in elementary school, I took them to church early in the morning on Ash Wednesday. As Roman Catholics, we were reminded by the parish priest on entering the season of Lent that "from dust we come, and to dust we shall return." This reminder, as Catholics know, was signified by a thumb-smudge of ashes on our foreheads. Customarily the ashes are not washed off during that day. However, when my children arrived at school, their teacher told them to "go wash your dirty foreheads." While they complied, my children also recognized the teacher's direction as a violation of their freedom of religious expression.

Some expressions of religion — such as active proselytizing or preaching — can be intrusive in the school setting, but most are not. Religious symbols — such as the wearing of a crucifix or a Star of David on a necklace, wearing a yarmulke on one's head, or wearing ashes on one's forehead on Ash Wednesday — usually are not intrusive. In fact, these nonintrusive examples are sufficiently common in American and Canadian society that they should be well-known by teachers. Thus asking Catholic children to wash their "dirty foreheads" is a trammeling of benign religious expression that is unnecessary and, indeed, unconstitutional. Nonacceptance in this form singles out students who are "different" from the mainstream in terms of religious belief and can be both harassing and alienating.

While Jewish, Catholic, and Protestant religious customs and symbols are fairly well-known in the United States and Canada, religious customs and symbols from non-Western cultures are less well-known. In some Southeast Asian religions, for example, the head is considered to be a "sacred temple." To pat someone on the head, therefore, is to commit an act of desecration. Thus, while the approving, affectionate patting of children's heads is a common, accepted practice in Western societies, it is a gesture reserved for parents (if for anyone) in certain Asian societies. When a teacher pats an Asian student on the head, that gesture, however well-meaning, may be interpreted as offensive.

Religion intertwines with culture when religion-based practices become associated with particular cultures, but that does not mean that everyone in that culture adheres to the primary religion's strictures. Over-generalization leads to stereotyping: Jews do not eat pork; all Mexicans are Catholic; all Arabs hate Jews. Some stereotypes seem to be innocent, while others are clearly divisive and destructive. But even innocent stereotypes can be hurtful when they single out individuals as "different," because in childhood, particularly, any difference can be magnified into a reason for teasing, shunning, or abusing.

Summary

To teach about diversity in a positive way — and to help children value, rather than denigrate, "difference" — educators first must become aware of the issues. Teachers and administrators must recognize the diversity around them and respond to that diversity before they can teach diverse students or teach students about that diversity. In the preceding sections I have tried to summarize the main diversity issues in terms of language development, socioeconomic status, stigma and resistance, learning style preferences, gender identity and sexual orientation, race and ethnicity, and religion. Of course, each of these areas might be explored at greater length — as they must be in circumstances where one or two types of issues predominate. These starting points should stimulate discussion and study.

Educators in the United States and Canada are becoming increasingly aware of and interested in diversity issues. Much has been made in the media of North America's "increasing diversity." I use this phrase in quotation marks because the populations of both Canada and the United States, both "nations of immigrants," always have been diverse. But recognition of such diversity is of more recent origin, brought about, in part, by population increases among minorities.

Canada has perhaps used more specific official language to recognize diversity than the United States. A bill passed by the Canadian House of Commons in 1988, for example, states:

> It is hereby declared to be the policy of the Government of Canada to recognize and promote the understanding; that multiculturalism reflects the cultural and racial diversity of Canadian society and acknowledges the freedom of all members of Canadian society to preserve, enhance, and share their cultural heritage. (House of Commons 1988)

Some would argue that such a policy is implicit in the United States, at least in certain areas of life. Others would point to wide disparity between the philosophy of preserving, enhancing, and sharing cultural heritages and the actions sometimes taken by government entities that reify a philosophy of preserving, enhancing, and imposing on everyone the dominant cultural heritage. For those who are not part of the dominant culture, the latter philosophy is denigrating and destructive. This is particularly true for children in schools.

Sensitivity to *diversity* (a term that I believe enlarges the notion of multiculturalism) can help educators to adopt educational strategies that make it possible for all children to realize their potential. In the words of Geneva Gay:

> Children who are secure in their identity, feel good about themselves, and are excited about what is happening in the classroom are more likely to engage eagerly in learning activities and achieve higher levels of academic performance than those who find the classroom hostile, unfriendly, insensitive, and perpetually unfamiliar. (1979, p. 327)

Chapter Three takes up the topic of instructional strategies that accommodate diversity. That discussion is followed, in Chapter Four, by a deeper plunge into the guiding forces of education, namely, curricula that reflect diversity. In some ways, it may be easiest to say that the next chapter examines what teachers can do singly — if necessary, individually. Chapter Four examines what educators can do collectively — by framing the "what" of teaching, not merely the "how."

Chapter Three

INSTRUCTIONAL STRATEGIES THAT ACCOMMODATE DIVERSITY

There is an old saying that if you give a man a fish, he will eat for a day; but if you teach a man to fish, he will never go hungry. That notion aptly captures the spirit of this chapter. The key word is *empowerment*, by which I mean that schools and teachers must empower students: to think for themselves; to construct knowledge, or meaning; and to learn respect for themselves and others.

To put this idea into action, I will begin by examining safety and equality as principles in working with student "differences." By "differences" I mean how students differ from one another as individuals; how student groups differ from one another; and, within the group context, how minorities differ from the majority. Next, I will discuss the theoretical bases for instruction that fosters true integration of individuals who are different from one another in terms of language, race, ethnicity, culture, and other factors. A necessary part of this discussion is an explication of facilitative teaching, which I take up in some detail. That discussion leads naturally into three specific areas of concern: behavior management, critical thinking, and cross-cultural interaction. These are particular areas in which instructional strategies that accommodate diversity are needed.

Safety and Equality

Schools and classrooms should be safe places for children and adolescents. That is a fundamental principle, which extends to the intellectual and the emotional, not merely to the physical. Of course, students should be kept safe from physical harm. But schools and classrooms also must keep students safe from mental harm — from stress, abuse, or harassment that prevents them from learning or threatens their emotional security.

Safe classrooms allow students to be themselves within the conventions of behavior; however, those "conventions" of behavior may vary because of cultural diversity. Thus cultural awareness, as I discussed in Chapter Two, is important for the teacher and administrator because such awareness can help them negotiate "conventions" and mediate conflicts that arise when so-called cultural norms are challenged. Two examples may illustrate this point.

First, in many Asian cultures it is considered impertinent, even aggressively rude, for a child to look directly at an adult's face. Submissively bowing one's head is the cultural norm of respect, particularly from a young person to an older person in authority. This is not the Western convention. Indeed, in Western societies the opposite is true. Children show respect by looking at the person who is speaking to them. When a teacher in an American or a Canadian classroom confronts an Asian immigrant student and says, "Look at me when I speak to you," the teacher is unwittingly demanding rudeness and defiance, not respect. Awareness of this convention of many Asian cultures can help teachers accommodate this "difference" and thereby avoid unnecessary conflict.

Another cultural "norm" is heterosexuality. But heterosexuality is not universal. Presuming that everyone is heterosexual is called *heterosexism*, which tends to exclude adolescents who may be gay or lesbian, who may be struggling to define their sexual orientation for themselves, or whose parent(s) may be gay or lesbian. (For convenience, I use the phrase "gay and lesbian," but it should be understood that other sexual variations are included, such as bisexuality and transgender.) Educators who are aware of such diversity are better able to make schools and classrooms safe places for students to be themselves, which includes being able to "be" gay or lesbian if that is their sexual orientation or to be open about their family life even when it differs from the "norm."

The companion to safety is equality. Students should have equal educational opportunities. To guarantee this end, it is essential to examine two facets of equality: *access* and *benefit*. The first is easier to achieve than the second.

When most people think about equal educational opportunity, they think about ensuring that all students have equal access to good schools, to high-quality instruction, to stimulating curricula, and so on. The struggle to provide such access for all children and adolescents in the United States and Canada has not been easy, nor has the goal been reached. Although much has changed for the better — for example, in the United States since the *Plessy* v. *Ferguson* days of "separate but equal" (a standard never achieved) — school districts everywhere still struggle to make equal access a reality.

But the counterpart to access is benefit. How can schools with diverse student populations ensure that all students can benefit equally from what the school has to offer? In other words, if a diverse student population is evidence that equal access has been achieved — all elements of the school are open to all students — then how can the school ensure that all students succeed on equal terms, that being part of a particular linguistic, racial, or ethnic group does not affect whether or not success in school is achieved? This is the question of equal benefit.

To answer this question successfully takes a thorough understanding of the diversity issues that I sketched in Chapter Two, coupled with a finer sense of equality. Too often, accommodating difference — let's say, linguistic difference — gets translated in classist or elitist terms. For example, when learners with limited English proficiency must tackle difficult texts, one approach can be to substitute simpler material, rather than to deal with the standard curriculum by using alternative instruction strategies, such as native-language translations and teaching methods that rely less on linguistic capability. I once worked in a high school where one of the English teachers often would say, "Why teach these poor kids Shakespeare? They can't even learn proper grammar. They'll certainly never be writers!" My counter was, "How do you know? Willa Cather, Ricardo Sanchez, and any number of other writers came from equally humble beginnings."

"Dumbing down" the curriculum *does* accommodate diversity after a fashion; however, it does not take equal benefit into account. This strategy is elitist (when the dominant culture imposes its standards on the nondominant without regard to difference), classist (when standards for students from middle- and upper-class families are different from standards for students from lower-class families), racist (when students of one race are treated better — given a richer curriculum, for example — than those of another race), and so on. These negative "-ists" are the treacherous waters of accommodation. Navigating them successfully takes both a keen understanding of diversity issues and a well-honed sense of equality of both access and benefit.

The key to achieving safety and equality is integration. I use the term *integration* to mean specifically the mixing of students — that is, the inclusion in the mainstream of students who are perceived to be somehow "different" from mainstream students. *Integration* shares linguistic roots with *integrity*, which is a useful way to remember that integration does not mean assimilation. Those who are assimilated give up (or simply lose) their home culture in order to join the mainstream culture. Integration means that those who join the mainstream retain their home culture; thus many cultures are mingled but retain individual integrity. In cliché terms, this is the patchwork quilt, not the melting pot.

Integration also is a philosophical and practical viewpoint that combats resistance culture. In Chapter Two I spoke of resistance culture as a defense mechanism by which those in an "oppressed" culture hang onto their home culture by rejecting assimilation

54

into the mainstream culture. Integration allows each individual to retain his or her cultural identity and to create, with everyone else, a larger culture of diversity. Ultimately, all of us participate in several cultures, at least in our home culture (which may itself be mixed) and in the larger, diverse culture that surrounds us at school or at work. Success comes from being able to move easily from culture to culture.

Theoretical Bases for Integration Strategies

It is not possible to discuss the theoretical bases for instruction that fosters true integration without also discussing how educators can empower students, ultimately, to be their own teachers. Students need to be taught to use the freedom that every individual possesses to think, to feel, and to act for oneself in order to achieve ends that are intrinsically worthwhile. The understanding of this freedom and its exercise are empowerment (Shor 1992).

In the practical world of the school and classroom, empowerment refers to helping students control and direct their feelings, thoughts, and actions to achieve socially constructive goals, in addition to learning and, one hopes, adopting the attitude of a lifelong learner. To empower students, however, requires that educators, to an extent, disempower themselves. By this I mean that teachers must step back from their traditional role of knowledge-giver and, instead, adopt the role of learning-enabler. I will try to put a finer point on this transition in roles.

The knowledge-giver role serves to perpetuate civilization — *a* civilization, to be specific. Knowledge from one age is passed along to the next; the civilization is replicated (albeit with some changes) from generation to generation through the process of knowledge-giving. But the capacity to pass on knowledge is necessarily limited. As knowledge expands, canons must be compiled so that the "best" knowledge is passed on and other information falls by the wayside.

The "knowledge explosion" has changed this way of thinking. Simply put, there is too much knowledge of use today. Canons are outmoded, because each culture has its own canon. Thus the question for schools becomes, Which canon? And perhaps the best answer is, All and none.

The alternative to knowledge-giving is learning-enabling. This is a constructivist notion of learning: Learners construct meaning, which is the knowledge that they will use in life. Two figures come to mind in the movement to transform teaching from knowledge-giving to learning-enabling: John Dewey and Paulo Freire.

John Dewey opposed teaching that fragmented knowledge into subject areas, arguing that the subject areas that made sense to adults did not necessarily make sense to young children. Young minds, Dewey suggested, do not fragment reality into discrete, therefore abstract, subjects. Rather, he argued, young minds deal with the immediate. Children learn holistically from experiences and by doing, rather than being told (Dewey 1938).

Dewey drew on his experiences with the laboratory school at the University of Chicago, which he ran at the turn of the century, for the articulation of his theories. Teachers in the school developed problem-solving lessons, experiments, and projects that were based not on a narrow canon, but on the curiosity and interests of their students. This grounding led to the development of the Progressive Education movement. However, by the 1930s the movement had lost steam and was being criticized for its lack of performance standards. Even Dewey was critical of interpreters of the movement and his pioneering work. The Great Depression and World War II diverted attention again to basic knowledge-giving designed to solidify the country (particularly the United States) and to stabilize the status quo. The 1950s and early 1960s did little to change this "practical" orientation.

The progressive spirit permutated and was revived in the late 1960s and 1970s. Paulo Freire challenged the knowledge-giver philosophy, for example, by calling it the "banking method" of teaching (Freire 1970). Teachers "bank" knowledge in the heads of their students, but the knowledge remains the property of the teacher. The students do not "own" the knowledge because they have not made it. In *Pedagogy of the Oppressed*, Freire contends that the "banking method" serves to oppress students because they are given the thoughts and feelings of others without being allowed to develop thoughts and feelings of their own. This leads them to think and act like others. They are dependent on teachers to "deposit" new knowledge. They are enslaved, rather than free.

Freire worked as a teacher in Brazil and other Latin American countries, where he experienced firsthand the oppressive nature of conventional, knowledge-giving instruction. He saw how schools treated ethnic minority peasants, compelling them to learn the state language and to adopt mainstream cultural values — and to discard their native language and culture. Many such students left school and remained illiterate, rather than give up their home culture. Freire was determined to approach such students in a different way.

Through question-and-answer strategies, Freire drew out his students. He discovered their experiences and interests. On this basis, over the course of six months, he was able to have his students reading and writing in their native language; this allowed them to develop knowledge (to make meaning) in terms that made sense to them. Once they could think for themselves, then they could benefit from mainstream schooling if they chose to do so. To Freire, liberation of mind — the ability to think for oneself or, in Freire's words, to achieve "critical consciousness" — should be the keystone of schooling.

In a time of political oppression, however, governments seldom want people to think for themselves, particularly if those people are ethnic minority peasants. Freire was exiled from his native land for teaching peasants to think for themselves. The same attitude once prevailed in the American South, where during the antebellum period it was illegal to teach black slaves how to read and write. Slave-state authorities feared that literate slaves — slaves who could think for themselves — would be more likely to rebel against their masters.

The teacher as learning-enabler, as I suggested a few paragraphs ago, is a constructivist view of teaching. Robert Slavin posed this definition:

Constructivism is a view of cognitive development as a process in which children actively build systems of meaning and understanding of reality through their experiences and interactions . . . children actively construct knowledge by continually assimilating and accommodating new information. (1994, p. 49)

Thus, to use the cliché, in constructivist teaching the teacher moves from being the "sage on the stage" to being a "guide on the side." The metaphor is teacher-as-coach.

It is easy to see why the transition from knowledge-giver to learning-enabler poses problems when one looks at the fundamental, historical sense of *teaching*. Teacher equates to "teller," one who *tells* or dispenses knowledge. In higher education, teachers are professors, those who "profess" or *declare* knowledge — and such knowledge is to be accepted, not disputed. Given this historical sense of what teachers *should* do, it is not difficult to understand both societal and personal reluctance to shed the knowledge-giver role. For teachers trained in the traditional role, moving to the side to serve as an intellectual/academic coach seems like shirking responsibility. Parents reared in the old school also sometimes wonder, "Why doesn't this teacher *teach*?"

Constructivist learning theory requires that educators reconceptualize the role of the teacher. (This often means that the roles of administrators and professors — the teachers of teachers — also must be reconceived.) The new concept can be sketched as follows:

Constructivist Assumptions:
• Meaning exists in every student's mind.
• Meaning is formed by individual experience.
• Learning occurs through social interaction.
• Students are responsible for their own learning.

Constructivist Environment:
• The classroom is a community of scholars.
• Learning is collaborative and cooperative.
• Teacher and students set high expectations for themselves.

Constructivist Teacher Role:
- The teacher sets the general curriculum.
- The teacher sets high achievement standards.
- The teacher facilitates and motivates learning from experience.

It may help to further clarify the constructivist position to say also what constructivist teaching is not. It is not *laissez faire*. The guide is on the side, not out of the room — or even on an equal level with the naive student. The *laissez faire* position, which is the true opposite of the knowledge-giver position, can be illustrated by a quick glance at the work of Jean Jacques Rousseau.

In Rousseau's 1762 book, *Émile*, the author described the education of a boy as *laissez faire*, meaning that there was little interference with or regulation of the boy's education by adults. Rousseau described the young child as a noble savage, a being full of pure thoughts and ideas (thus noble) but uncultivated to live in human society (thus savage). If a child is left to his own intuitions, he (or she) will grow up to be a good person. If a child is "corrupted" by society, then he or she will take on society's ills. Therefore, a "natural education," in which the child is watched over by adults who do not intrude on the child's quest for knowledge, would prevent such corruption and be the best form of education.

Such "natural education" has had some appeal, though few education theorists have taken the notion as far as Rousseau would have it taken. Frederick Froebel adopted aspects of natural education in his concept of the *kindergarten*, the child in the garden. Closer to the present, A.S. Neill (1960) adopted Rousseau's model for his Summerhill school, where children and adults "negotiated" the nature and shape of the school community and children carved out their own self-directed learning experiences from the environment around them with little, if any, assistance from the adults.

Natural education, or *laissez faire* education, does not meet the standards of constructivist teaching because it omits adult assistance. Constructivist theory is predicated on facilitative teaching, in which the teacher acts as a coach or facilitator of learning for students. Facilitative teaching includes both didactic, direct instruction and "guide on the side," indirect instruction. The sports coach is an appropriate model. Coaches of sports use direct instruction to impart important knowledge; learners incorporate such information into their own knowledge base, modifying existing understandings to create new meaning; then coaches move aside and allow learners to apply and practice those new understandings, providing correction and advice as needed.

For example, it would be a silly waste of time to expect students simply to discover the rules of tennis, how to hold a tennis racket, and so on. This knowledge is best conveyed through direct instruction. But learning directly how to hold and swing a tennis racket is only the beginning. Students also must learn how to connect with the ball, how to hit the ball over the net, in short, how to play the game practically (physically) *after* they have learned how to play the game theoretically (rules and procedures). Actually playing the game requires the teacher to get out of the way — to teach indirectly by coaching from the sidelines.

Facilitative teaching allows and encourages the student to become self-directed. The student-as-player is active, rather than passive. Thus the student gains what Freire called "critical consciousness," the capacity to make one's own decisions and to have thoughts and feelings that are not dictated by the teacher. This manner of instruction is well-suited to teaching for diversity because it provides a framework for instruction within which students are more likely to be able to be themselves, to feel safe in being themselves, and to derive equal benefit from instruction to which they and their peers have access.

I began this section by saying that integration strategies must be premised on empowering students. Ultimately, that is the end sought by facilitative teaching. Teachers who facilitate student learning empower students to become their own teachers and to use well their personal freedom to think, to feel, and to act for themselves. In the sections that follow I will delve deeper into the application of facilitative instruction in contexts that give substance to theoretical notions of empowerment and teaching for diversity.

Facilitative Teaching in Action

As I suggested in the previous section, facilitative teaching mixes direct and indirect instruction — just as coaching does — but the emphasis is on helping students to construct knowledge. Another way to think about facilitative teaching is to consider a continuum of instructional strategies. Facilitative teaching strategies range from the convergent to the divergent.

Facilitative teaching that is convergent:
• is product-directed;
• seeks limited responses;
• focuses on teacher-selected skills and knowledge; and
• helps students analyze and synthesize provided information.

Facilitative teaching that is divergent:
• is process-directed;
• seeks open responses;
• focuses on student-selected skills and knowledge; and
• helps students discover information to be analyzed and synthesized.

An illustration may help to make this notion of a continuum more concrete. Mrs. Kelly is a mathematics teacher. She decides that her students should learn about economies of scale. Her first approach is more toward the convergent end of the continuum. She directly teaches students the definition of "economy of scale" — simply stated, that large-scale buying often can make the unit price lower than if the same units were bought singly or on a smaller scale. Then Mrs. Kelly poses a problem: Is it cheaper for a consumer to make six hamburgers by buying all the ingredients in the grocery and making the hamburgers at home or by purchasing six ready-made hamburgers at a local fast-food restaurant? What economy of scale is at work.

The students work up two sets of figures. This part of the lesson is still more convergent than divergent but moving along the continuum toward the divergent end.

The first set is for the hamburger ingredients from the grocery: meat ($2.15), buns ($1.10), pickles (25¢), onions (75¢), ketchup (99¢). The total for six hamburgers comes to $5.24. The second set of figures is for six hamburgers purchased at the fast-food restaurant: 6 x 99¢ each = $5.94.

Now the lesson moves to the divergent end of the continuum. What questions are raised by these two sets of figures? Certainly, it appears to be cheaper to make one's own hamburgers — if one is willing to put in the labor to do so. But what about overhead? The homemade hamburgers also require a kitchen, utensils, gas or electric heat, and so on.

The average cost of a homemade hamburger is 87¢ *for the ingredients only*. The average price of the fast-food hamburger is 99¢, but that price also includes both overhead costs and profit. Through analysis — thinking about "hidden" costs and asking questions about additional factors — students can arrive at the conclusion that the fast-food restaurant probably buys its ingredients for much less than the grocery prices. In addition to being able to buy at wholesale prices (another factor that students can discover), a major factor in the restaurant's favor is economy of scale: The restaurant is buying enough ingredients to make not just six hamburgers, but probably several hundred.

Once students arrive at this conclusion, they have met the goal of the lesson. In other words, they have used some divergent strategies to meet the teacher's (convergent) goal of understanding economy of scale. However, the students might continue to take the lesson in a divergent direction by connecting this lesson to other questions *they* want to investigate, such as, Which local fast-food restaurants offer the most hamburger for the money? If homemade hamburgers actually cost more when factors in addition to ingredients are considered, what are some other reasons why people might still want to make their own hamburgers? The students also might introduce ethnic or cultural twists. For example, How do hamburger costs compare to the costs associated with making tacos or burritos?

My point is that facilitative teaching, as illustrated in this example from Mrs. Kelly's math class, offers a range of ways both to reach the teacher's lesson goals and to encourage students to think and learn based on their own needs and interests.

Previously, I sketched four constructivist assumptions: Meaning exists in every student's mind; meaning is formed by individual experience; learning occurs through social interaction; and students are responsible for their own learning. Those assumptions can be expanded as follows:

- Students have a natural propensity for learning and are curious about the world.
- Curiosity and interest are high when students believe that learning activities are relevant to their needs and interests.
- Students need help to deal with information that conflicts with what they already know or challenges their prior understandings.
- Experiential learning activities are most effective when guidance is available to help students integrate new knowledge with prior knowledge.
- Active learning is most effective when students are allowed and encouraged to frame the learning challenge and to decide how to address it.
- Self-evaluation promotes self-reliance, independence, and creativity, which are important to develop autonomy as a learner.
- Openness to change and a willingness to examine new ideas are fundamental to lifelong learning.

In summary, I suggest that teachers consider the following guidelines for facilitative teaching that balances the convergent with the divergent:

1. Create a climate, a context, and a set of conditions to allow students to pursue their own curiosities.
2. Identify and clarify the general purposes for the learning activity.

3. Assist students to identify and clarify their individual purposes within the learning activity.
4. Organize a wide array of resources for the students or teach them how to use the library, data banks, museums, and so on.
5. Become a resource to their students and share knowledge and experiences.
6. Be alert to feelings that are expressed by students and adjust the structure of instruction accordingly.
7. Accept personal limitations (teachers do not have to know everything).
8. Model attitudes of a lifelong learner.
9. Intervene when students get stuck or waste time.

Having laid a foundation for instruction that accommodates diversity, I now turn to some specific areas of concern: behavior management, critical thinking, and cross-cultural interaction. While I will treat these areas separately, it also should be clear that they overlap and interconnect. The strategies that I suggest in the following sections are based on the premise that facilitative teaching with an emphasis on the teacher's role as learning-enabler should be woven into the fabric of instruction, whether the goal is to help students become autonomous learners or critical thinkers or to encourage positive, rewarding cross-cultural interaction.

Behavior Management

Behavior management — or classroom discipline — often becomes a heightened concern when teachers encourage students to think and to act on their own initiative. This is true in a class that is mostly homogeneous; it becomes even more of a factor when the class makeup is highly diverse. How can teachers address the concern for good discipline without becoming authoritarian and directive? Or how can they balance facilitative, nondirective teaching with behavior management that may, at times, require control and direction? And how can teachers maintain good classroom discipline, encourage autonomy, and deal positively with cultural differences simultaneously?

The answer to all of these questions mainly lies in helping students balance two factors of their own: autonomy and self-control. In the preceding sections I have placed a great deal of emphasis on helping students to become autonomous learners. The companion to autonomy is self-control. Autonomy carries the notion of freedom — freedom to learn, freedom to choose subjects and methods of study, and so on. However, no freedom is absolute. Autonomy must be tempered by self-control, which means that students choose what and how to learn within certain limits.

Part of self-control is developed through teacher direction. Within facilitative teaching, certain elements will be convergent: teacher-determined goals, direct instruction, and so on. Students learn a measure of self-control through observing the teacher's examples. Another part of self-control comes from external expectations — from parents, from the community, from society in general.

But a key part of the development of self-control is the student's sense of self. That sense of self can be encouraged or discouraged by the responses of the teacher and the student's peers to the student's appearance, speech, family background, religious beliefs, and so on. In short, the student's sense of self is linked to his or her feelings of acceptance. Such acceptance is perceived on several levels: self-acceptance, peer acceptance, acceptance by parents and significant others, teacher acceptance, and acceptance by the world in general.

Belief in oneself, or self-acceptance, is perhaps the most important of these perceptions. It often is tied to a belief that one can produce an effect. Psychologists call this *self-efficacy*. For example, clinical psychologists have found that the alcoholics most likely to give up alcohol and stay sober are those who genuinely *believe* that they can do so. Belief in the ability to control one's actions is a strong part of self-control — and it goes hand-in-hand with feelings of autonomy as a learner. A student's sense of self-efficacy can be increased or decreased by actions and attitudes within a classroom. When feelings of self-efficacy are decreased, self-control also will likely decrease.

Diminished self-control can lead to inappropriate behavior, which is a management problem both for the teacher — because the student's actions may interfere with other students' learning or the teacher's ability to teach — and for the student, whose own ability to learn is diminished. One response to diminished self-control is to impose greater external control — that is, for the teacher to move to the convergent end of the continuum, becoming more authoritarian, more directive. But this response is likely to be effective only in the short term. The better response — and the only response likely to succeed in the long term — is to investigate the source of the student's diminished sense of self-efficacy and to work to solve that problem.

Because self-efficacy is built on beliefs about what one can do (in other words, the effect one can produce), teachers can build self-efficacy by helping students to do four things:

Set realistic goals and standards. Maria is a student in a swimming class. She wants to be an Olympic swimmer, but she just started swimming at the age of 15. Although it is unlikely that Maria will ever qualify for the Olympic team, it would be unfair to dismiss her dream ("Oh, Maria, you'll never make it!"). On the other hand, it would be equally unfair to be mindlessly optimistic ("Maria, you can do anything you put your mind to."). Maria needs help setting realistic goals — goals that may or may not lead to the Olympics — but goals that can be achieved. For example, a reasonable goal might be to try out for the swim team at school or at the local swim club. Realistic goals and standards are more likely than "pie in the sky" goals to lead to solid achievements that build the student's sense of self-efficacy. In Maria's case, realistic goals that are met also may lead to a lifelong love of swimming, to a college swimming scholarship, and, just maybe, to the Olympics.

Direct behavior toward achievement. Many students set goals for themselves but then fail to follow through. Achievement takes action; it takes doing, not just thinking. When Maria sets her goal as joining the local swim club, she also needs to be guided to think about how that goal can be achieved. Will it require a certain amount of practice? When will that practice be done? Will practice be enhanced by changes in diet or sleeping patterns? To build self-efficacy, Maria may need guidance to discover the details that will best chart her path to goal achievement. Facilitative teaching can be used to help Maria make the necessary discoveries — and also to learn how to think about goal-fulfillment in proactive ways in other situations.

Assess achievement and adjust direction. Maria has difficulty with the butterfly-stroke lap of a swim relay. She feels like a failure. To distinguish herself and get on the swim team, she must improve her butterfly stroke. The thoughtful teacher (in the role of coach) will recognize — and help Maria to recognize — that achievement is earned in stages. Maria is assessing her own achievement when she recognizes that she needs to work on her butterfly stroke. But the assumption of failure is unproductive. The teacher needs to help her understand that this need is not a failure — nor is *she* a failure because she has this need. Improving the butterfly stroke is a realistic goal. Once Maria realizes this, she can adjust the direction of her efforts by defining (for herself) the steps it will take to achieve her goal of improving her butterfly stroke.

Redirect goals based on achievement. What happens after a goal is achieved? The easy answer is, Set another goal. Indeed, achievement of one goal often reveals a new goal. Maria realizes her goal of making the swim team. That is an achievement to be celebrated. But that achievement also reveals another goal: to be the best swimmer (or one of the best) on the team, for example.

This four-step goal process is a form of behavior management. By engaging in this process with students, teachers can help students balance autonomy with self-control, because they have a direction to take. And that direction leads to stronger feelings of self-efficacy.

Following are some general suggestions for taking these steps into the academic environment:

- Ask students to compile a list of skills they want to master. Help them prioritize their list.
- Help students develop goals related to their priorities; break large goals into more workable pieces.
- Work with students to develop action plans that will guide the students to the achievement of their goals. Set up timelines for achievement.
- Encourage students to re-examine their goals periodically, assess their progress, and readjust their goals as needed.
- Celebrate goal attainment, and help students base new goals on goals they have already achieved.

Students with low self-efficacy will present the greatest behavioral management challenges. Insecurity about one's value in the eyes of oneself and others, feelings of oppression and rejection, can lie behind some students' need to act out, to defy authority, or, conversely, to withdraw from social interaction. Students who are "different" in some way from mainstream students are more likely to express feelings of low self-efficacy than are students who consider themselves to be part of the mainstream, regardless of the actual composition of the mainstream. This is to say that in a diverse (heterogeneous) mainstream, some students still are likely to perceive themselves as "different."

Critical Thinking

Under the rubric of critical thinking I also include what Dewey called "reflective thinking," which means thinking that involves doubt and resolution. That is the type of thinking, in fact, that I want to address first. Schrag refers to such thinking as a "disposition toward thoughtfulness" (1988, p. 8). Dewey wrote:

> [R]eflective thinking . . . involves (1) a state of doubt, hesitation, perplexity, mental difficulty, in which thinking originates, and (2) an act of searching, hunting, inquiring to

find material that will solve the doubt, settle and dispose of the perplexity. (1933, p. 12)

Implicit in Dewey's definition and in Shrag's phrase is the idea that reflective thinking involves shedding preconceptions and, if you will, prejudices. This is an important concept in teaching for diversity, because ingrained preconceptions and prejudices about individuals who are "different" get in the way of clear thinking.

As an introduction to reflective thinking for teachers in training, I use a scenario such as the one that follows to help my students consider not only basic classroom management problems but also how such problems are affected by issues of diversity.

Niki Buska and the Lunch Bag

Niki Buska, a sixth-grader, had been transferred from her lower-class neighborhood school to an upper-middle-class neighborhood school as part of the school district's desegregation effort. Niki's father works in an iron foundry, and Niki has little in common with her classmates, most of whose fathers work in offices. Niki also differs from her classmates in the language she uses, which is tinged with "street tough." And Niki often speaks up without raising her hand to get the teacher's permission. But, for the most part, Niki is a quiet student and does not bother anyone.

One day as the students are preparing to go to lunch, Dick speaks up.

Dick: Mrs. Brooks, someone stole my lunch!
Mrs. Books: Where was your lunch, Dick?
Dick: Right here, under my desk in a brown bag.
Mrs. Brooks: What did you have in it?
Dick: I had two bologna sandwiches — with ketchup.
Niki: Bologna with ketchup. Yuk!
Dick: I like ketchup! There was a bag of cookies in it, too.
Jane: Mrs. Brooks, I saw Niki take his bag.
Niki: No way! I don't like bologna with ketchup!
Sally: I saw Niki stick the bag under her desk.

Mrs. Brooks: Niki, let me have your lunch bag.

Niki: Hey, buzz off! I got rights!

Mrs. Brooks: Now, Niki, give me the bag!

Mrs. Brooks grabs Niki's bag. As Niki tries to jerk it away, the bag rips and onto the floor spills Niki's lunch: two tacos and an apple. Also, on the floor are two bologna sandwiches and a bag of cookies.

Niki: Hey, you spilled my lunch all over the floor!

Mrs. Brooks: Well! The nerve. There's Dick lunch, too!

Niki: I don't know how it got in my bag, Mrs. Brooks. I ain't lying.

Mrs. Brooks: I don't know what to do with you, Niki. We've tried hard to get along with you. Now you steal Dick's lunch.

Niki: I didn't take it! I don't even like bologna and ketchup!

Mrs. Brooks: Well, the rest of us are going to lunch now. Dick, I'll get you a hot lunch in the cafeteria. Niki, by the time we get back, I want this mess cleaned up. You'll have time to think about telling the truth.

The other students and Mrs. Brooks proceed to the cafeteria, while Niki stays behind in the classroom.

Scenarios such as this one are helpful in working with students at all levels, because such scenes are rich in interpretive possibilities.* Indeed, this scenario could easily be used in elementary, middle school, or high school classes.

Setting aside consideration of the basic classroom management issues for the moment, I ask my prospective teachers to consider the diversity issues at work in this scenario. What are the cultural dynamics of this situation? Does socioeconomic class affect this scene? Would Mrs. Brooks have reacted differently if, say, Sally or Jane were accused of stealing? Was Niki "framed"?

---

*For a short primer on using scenarios, see Violet Anselmini Allain and Alvin M. Pettus, *Teaching Diverse Students: Preparing with Cases*, Fastback 429 (Bloomington, Ind.: Phi Delta Kappa Educational Foundation, 1998).

Why might that happen? And what prejudices might Mrs. Brooks be displaying in her handling of this incident?

Becoming autonomous learners requires that students become critical thinkers, and using scenarios is one strategy that not only can accommodate diverse viewpoints but also can help students to consider the dynamics of diversity at work in social and learning situations. Scenarios are most effective in encouraging reflective thinking.

Another way to view critical thinking is to look at solving problems. Richard Paul commented, "If there is no problem, there is no point in thinking critically" (1993, p. 91). When humans attempt to solve problems, critical thinkers usually go about the task by using divergent or convergent strategies. *Divergent* thinking refers to creating ideas. Brainstorming and free association are divergent thinking strategies. By creating ideas freely, a solution (or more than one solution) may be found for a problem. *Convergent* thinking, in contrast, refers to assessing ideas and making judgments. Weighing pros and cons and looking "behind" the ideas to find their merits are strategies of convergent thinking. Divergent and convergent strategies often are used in tandem to solve problems.

Ultimately, critical thinking is about arriving at judgments. Did the teacher behave fairly? Was the solution to the problem appropriate? To arrive at a sound judgment, it is necessary to investigate three questions, which tend to be the same questions whether a perplexing situation requires reflection or a problem needs to be solved:

- What do I want to know?
- How can I find the answer?
- How do I know the answer is any good?

These questions can be approached in a number of ways. The five most commonly recognized ways of knowing are: authority (relying on expert opinion), intuition (listening to one's inner voice), reason (applying logic), experiment (testing theories or possible solutions), and observation (relying on the senses). The

71

following paragraphs examine each of these ways of knowing with reference to teaching for diversity.

Authority. Teachers and parents are the primary "authorities" in students' lives. However, authority is never infallible; and particularly in Western societies, students are taught from early on to question authority — long before the rebellious questioning of adolescence. While teachers and parents sometimes resent such questioning, most also realize that is it endemic to Western culture. But that is not the case in every culture. Students from non-Western cultures respond differently to authority and in many cases may be (at least outwardly) more subservient to authority.

Attitudes toward authority affect classroom management in obvious ways; however, they also affect how students respond to instruction and how they interact with the curriculum. Teachers who have had an opportunity to teach in China or Japan, for example, often report how difficult it is to get their students to ask questions or participate in discussions, because questioning the teacher or expressing a personal opinion can be viewed as challenging authority, which is culturally inappropriate. This attitude can be a hurdle to overcome in helping students from non-Western backgrounds to become autonomous learners, because critical thinking requires the thinker to challenge authority.

Another facet of the authority issue is resistance to authority. Students who view the mainstream culture as different from their own may resist authority that they see as trying to rob them of their own culture. Recall resistance culture, which I discussed in Chapter Two. Students who reject authority as a way of knowing will likely have difficulty attaining what Freire called "critical consciousness." Just as mainstream students must be open to diversity that calls on them to consider authorities outside the sphere of their home culture, so also must students who are somehow "different" be willing to consider mainstream authorities, who are outside their home culture.

Intuition. Listening to one's "inner voice" is another way of knowing. Whether intuition is referred to as "conscience" or "common sense," it is informed by experience. Intuition is not genetic; it is the product of one's upbringing. And that upbringing is contained within various contexts: cultural, economic, social, religious, and so on. What teachers and other learning-enablers must realize is the enormous diversity of such contexts. Thus a "commonsense solution" to a problem may not be universal.

At the same time, it must be said that a certain degree of universality can be anticipated *within* some contexts. A couple of historical examples may be useful. One need only recall that early peoples believed that the sun circled the earth. Common sense coupled with observation of the sun "rising" in the east and "setting" in the west led to this wholly inaccurate belief. In much the same way, people once believed the earth was flat. After all, from observation it certainly *seemed* flat. But, again, common sense was wrong. In both cases it took scientists — critical thinkers — who were willing to question prevailing knowledge, to question so-called common sense, and to examine their intuition, to correct the intuitive knowledge.

To take such questioning into a diversity context, consider the act of giving a gift. When someone gives you a gift, intuition (or common sense) would seem to say that it is appropriate to respond by giving that person a gift, too. In many cultures, *exchanging* gifts is a cultural norm. But that "norm" is not universal. Among some Native Americans, for example, exchanging gifts amounts to a form of commerce; it reduces "giving" to "trading." A true gift is just that — something given without thought of any return or reciprocation. And so reciprocation among these Native Americans is viewed not only as unnecessary but as downright rude.

In summary, intuition is a way of knowing within a cultural context. Critical thinking, however, often requires the thinker to question intuition, just as the critical thinker also must question authority.

Reason. The application of logic also depends on other ways of knowing. For example, if I wonder whether I have enough gas

73

to get to another town, I can apply a mathematical formula. I have to travel 60 miles. My car has three gallons of gasoline in it, and the car gets 20 miles to the gallon. Mathematical logic says, yes, I will make it to the other town. But mathematical logic alone is seldom useful in real life. Reason requires the application of more than pure mathematics. If the town 60 miles away lies downhill, I may have more than enough gas. But if it lies uphill, I made not have enough gas. And what about wind? A headwind also would lower my car's gas mileage; a tailwind could raise it.

Pure, or abstract, logic is insufficient for effective reasoning in human situations. Moreover, "common logic" is culture-bound in many cases. Thus reason must take into account the cultural contexts at hand. It once seemed "reasonable" to bleed sick people for all kinds of ailments, but we now understand that bleeding is more often counterproductive than helpful. At the same time, Western medical professionals once viewed the commonplace Asian practice of acupuncture as "illogical" — as "folk medicine" in its most derogatory connotation. However, acupuncture now is being considered seriously, and in some quarters accepted, as a legitimate medical practice by Western authorities.

Reason as a way of knowing, like authority and intuition, must be considered in light of cultural factors. Students must learn that bases for reasoning vary from context to context, and what may be "logical" in one setting may be viewed as "illogical" in another setting.

Experiment. Another way of knowing is to experiment. In my previous example, instead of relying on reason to decide whether I could drive 60 miles on three gallons of gasoline, I might conduct an experiment, or even a series of experiments. For example, I might conduct some trials in which I change certain variables, such as wind and driving speed. In this way I might discover that, yes, three gallons is sufficient *if* there is a tailwind of X miles per hour or *if* I drive no faster than X mph.

Experiments offer ways to investigate ideas, or theories. But experimentation is likely to have ethical, moral, or legal limitations, which are the artifacts of culture. Naturally, such limitations differ from culture to culture. For example, some students will find certain experiments with animals morally reprehensible, while others with less reverence for animals will find the desire to obtain accurate, scientific knowledge a compelling reason for animal experiments.

Cultural issues that surround experiment as a way of knowing generally do not concern scientific methods; rather, they focus on the purposes and components of experimentation. In effectively teaching for diversity, therefore, it is important to consider the cultural ramifications of a proposed experiment. Even an experiment as simple as discovering whether or not three gallons of gasoline are sufficient to drive 60 miles may be questionable if, as in a strict Amish community, driving itself is considered to be taboo.

Observation. The old saying is, "Seeing is believing." Observation as a way of knowing requires that one specify what is to be looked for and how such observations are to be noted, catalogued, and evaluated. But *how* one observes — what one chooses to see or to ignore and what one makes of what is seen — often is influenced by cultural factors. Factors such as race, sex, sexual orientation, religion, and ethnicity are the lenses through which humans make observations.

Return to the scenario of Niki Buska, for example, and assume that Niki is Hispanic. Two stereotypes illustrate this notion of cultural lenses. For example, a stereotypical white observer with certain ethnic and classist prejudices might observe this scene and conclude that Niki *is* a thief and a liar. After all, she is poor and Hispanic — two strikes against her — and probably comes from a family and community in which such behavior is considered typical, perhaps even acceptable. On the other hand, a stereotypical Hispanic observer with certain ethnic and classist prejudices might conclude the opposite: Someone framed Niki, probably those snobbish white girls in her class, because that is how whites always treat Hispanics, especially poor ones. Of course, both of these are extreme (though not unheard of) views.

But my point is that observation is not value-free. Indeed, it is value-laden, and those values often are based on cultural factors that are not universal.

Teaching students to be critical thinkers requires teachers to help students achieve, in Shrag's phrase, a "disposition toward thoughtfulness." In teaching for diversity it is especially important, therefore, to emphasize habits of thought that avoid certain pitfalls. Such pitfalls include:

- Bias. Preconceptions and prejudices narrow the lens of perception. One's perceptions form the primary screens to interpret reality. Biased perception is selective and prevents the consideration of new ideas.
- Stereotyping. When bias is generalized to a group (type), then misconceptions are perpetuated and new information is closed out. Stereotyping obscures the individual. (A worthwhile example of a study in stereotyping for students who are good readers is Ralph Ellison's novel, *The Invisible Man*.)
- Absolutes. Rigid, categorical thinking obscures nuances of meaning. Either-or thinking, or black-and-white thinking, blocks out essential ambiguity. Absolutes exist in the abstract, rarely in the concrete.

In summary, effective critical thinkers: 1) ask penetrating questions that go beyond biases and stereotypes; 2) defer judgment to avoid jumping to conclusions before all possibilities have been considered and all information has been gathered; 3) consider a wide array of options, ideas, and solutions, examining them through eyes that are sensitive to cultural issues; and 4) look for connections between new and existing knowledge and understanding, knowing that such connections are how meaning is constructed.

In this section I have tried to touch on critical thinking issues that have a particular bearing on teaching for diversity. Clearly, critical thinking could be — and has been — the subject of entire books. My goal has been simply to provide a starting point for thinking about critical thinking as a key component of teaching for diversity — by which I mean both teaching diverse students how to get along and, indeed, how to benefit from interactions with one another, as well as teaching all students how to live in a diverse world.

Cross-Cultural Interaction

The final area of concern that I want to take up in this chapter on instructional strategies that accommodate diversity is cross-cultural interaction. In the introduction to *Education for Cultural Pluralism: Global Roots Stew*, I explained that fastback's subtitle by saying:

> *Global roots stew* represents three human concerns: *Global* represents the concern of thinking and acting as citizens of one planet, Earth. *Roots* represents the concern of being connected with the past. *Stew* represents the concern of belonging to a harmonious society while retaining a unique identity. (1981, p. 6)

In Chapter One I discussed the notion of *viability*. The role of education is to produce "viable" individuals. Viable individuals are capable of sustaining an intellectual life, of growing and developing mentally. The notion of a "global roots stew" speaks directly to cultural viability.

While it can be argued that students do not automatically become viable individuals within their home culture — that nurturing and teaching are necessary there, too, and usually done by parents and other significant members of the family or cultural community — the main task of teaching for diversity is to assist students to become viable individuals *across cultures*. What does it take for students to function effectively outside their home culture?

Immigrants to the New World 150 years ago might have retained their home cultures more easily than they can today. Transportation and communication were more difficult then. Communities often remained fairly self-contained. Major cities and many small towns were composed of such cultural enclaves, in which the inhabitants might continue to speak their native language, perhaps never learning English at all. The remnants of these early communities can be seen today in places like New York and Chicago — enclaves such as Greektown, Chinatown, Little Italy, and so on.

A hundred years ago, roughly speaking, American (and, to a lesser extent, Canadian) society began to shift toward assimilation: the melting pot. In a melting pot one places bits of different metals: gold, silver, copper. All are melted together, losing their individual characteristics and becoming an amalgam. To be a true American, the melting-pot notion went, one gave up one's home culture and language and adopted the culture and language of mainstream America, or at least an idealized, Norman Rockwell kind of American mainstream.

However, assimilation created problems. Second-generation immigrant children grew up learning only English, and soon grandparents were unable to talk to grandchildren because they spoke different languages. Traditional customs were set aside; children adopted "American" customs, dress, and manners, often to the dismay of their parents and grandparents. Generation gaps became cultural gaps as well.

The notion of a "global roots stew" as an alternative to assimilation began about 40 years ago. *Multiculturalism* is the common term; the metaphors are the patchwork quilt, the cultural salad, the global roots stew. All are apt. In a stew the ingredients work together, each lending its essence to the savory broth of the larger community. At the same time, the ingredients also retain their individual identities: the potatoes are still potatoes, not carrots or onions or beef. Thus in the diversity of a multicultural society, individuals learn how to communicate and work with one another across cultures. They find common ground. But they do not become one another; they retain their individual cultural identities.

Multicultural communities, such as schools and classrooms, must balance the needs of the common society against the needs of diverse individuals and subgroups within the community. Viability must be nurtured against a backdrop of diversity. But individuals who are like-minded, for want of a better term — for example, of the same race, the same ethnicity, the same sex — tend to coalesce. A general term for this phenomenon is *ethnocentrism*, which is most associated with ethnic group cohesiveness, as the term suggests.

While ethnocentrism often is spoken of in negative terms, I will argue that there is "good" ethnocentrism as well as "bad" ethnocentrism. At root, *ethnocentrism* means simply to focus, or "center," on one's own culture, usually expressed in ethnic terms (hence *ethno-*) but now often broadened to include other factors, such as gender, class, and race. Ethnocentrism can range from *arrogance* at one extreme to *degradation* at the other.

Arrogant ethnocentrism is the view that one's group is superior to all others, that the group can do no wrong. During the rise of Nazi Germany, to cite an extreme example, Aryan nationalism was arrogant ethnocentrism. And on a milder (though still virulent) level, arrogant ethnocentrism is expressed whenever one group oppresses or restricts another from a belief in their own, supposed superiority over that other group.

The opposite end of the ethnocentrism continuum is degradation. Ethnocentric degradation is the belief that one's own group is inferior to others. Many minority groups, consistently bombarded by the negative stereotypes foisted on them by others, struggle against feelings of ethnocentric degradation. As a youngster, to give a personal example, I was caught up from time to time in the negative stereotyping of Hispanics as lazy, cruel, or dishonest. Children can be affected by degradation in the ways their ethnic group is portrayed in the media. I recall the Frito Bandito commercials of the 1960s as a form of stereotyping. Others may recall an earlier period in which the radio and television versions of *Amos 'n' Andy* stereotyped African Americans as shiftless and stupid.

Both arrogant ethnocentrism and ethnocentric degradation are "bad" ethnocentrism. In the middle of the continuum, however, is a range of "good" ethnocentrism. This middle ground can be

79

expressed as *legitimate group pride*. Often minority groups center on a holiday observance — or create a celebration — to foster group pride as a way of combating negative stereotyping by the majority or other groups. One recalls the slogan, "Black is Beautiful," which found its way into advertising, as did "You've come a long way, baby," which resounded during the women's rights movement. "Gay Pride" days in June each year are celebrated in cities across the United States. And every March St. Patrick's Day celebrations are focused on Irish pride, though the long history of their observance mutes the distant memory of Irish immigrant stereotyping: "micks" as slow-witted, lazy, and dishonest.

Group pride celebrations provide an opportunity not only for group members to demonstrate that they are proud of who they are but also for group members and observers to learn more about the group. Over the years I have learned, for example, about Hispanics who have fought in every U.S. war since the Civil War — and earned 37 Congressional Medals of Honor. I have learned of Hero Street, U.S.A., in Silvis, Illinois, which was named to memorialize eight Mexican-American heroes who lived on that street and gave their lives in defense of their country.

Group pride celebrations also become family celebration times. Group pride and family pride are mingled, sometimes specifically, by groups such as PFLAG, in which the initials stand for Parents, Family and Friends of Lesbians and Gays. In my own family I have discovered interesting history: a distant uncle who had fought for the North in the Civil War Battle of Glorieta Canyon in New Mexico, a brother who fought in World War II, and two other family members who served in the U.S. Marines. Knowing the best about one's family often blends with knowing the best about one's group, and the product is legitimate group pride.

One objective of cross-cultural interaction is to foster recognition and value for legitimate group pride, in terms both of one's own cultural group and of other groups. That recognition and value must begin with teachers and administrators before it can be transmitted to students. Such recognition often starts with seeing one's own prejudices. I recall a colleague saying, "I don't notice that my new students are black or white. To me, they are all as white as I am." He was sincerely trying to be "colorblind," trying to treat all students equally without regard to race; but what he didn't realize was his unwitting prejudice. "They are all as white as I am" says that being "white" is superior.

Another example: A teacher commented in the faculty lounge, "Mary and Sally want to organize a club for gay and lesbian students. [embarrassed giggle] They asked me to be the sponsor. I told them I was 100% female. [giggle] I mean, sometimes I wish I were a man to know how it feels, but. . . . Anyway, I told them I would be glad to be their sponsor." Clearly, the teacher was embarrassed by the suggestion, which she took to be implicit, that she might be suited to sponsor the club if she had any lesbian feelings — if she wanted to be a man, in her understanding. Although her agreement to sponsor the club is well-intentioned, she is uncomfortable with the "difference" being expressed by Mary and Sally and, as is painfully clear, is unfamiliar with what it means to be a lesbian.

Equal education is not about becoming colorblind but about treating all students equally, which includes extending equal regard for each student's culture. Effective cross-cultural interaction must start with learning about different cultures, as I suggested in Chapter Two. Thus for educators and their students, cross-cultural interaction must begin with openness. Students must be encouraged to share their culture, not just in a "heroes and holidays" approach but at a deeper level. Following are three general strategies for enhancing awareness and fostering communication and cross-cultural interaction.

Exposure and Cooperation. Students need to learn about one another's cultures in both formal and informal ways. They can learn directly about other cultures through research and reading and other formal classroom activities. Teachers can structure student exchanges and cultural field trips. They can invite guests into the classroom. Such basic knowledge-building strategies are most helpful when they encompass not only the cultural representation of the classroom but also cultures not represented in the classroom. This is especially true in schools and classrooms that are largely homogeneous, where teachers may not feel any particular urgency to promote cross-cultural awareness and interaction. However, students in all-black, all-white, all-Hispanic, or all-Asian classrooms are going to live in a world that is multicultural. They need to be able to function across cultures just as much as students who go to school in multicultural classrooms.

Informal learning comes about from casual contact. Working together in cooperative groups, for example, is a way for students to come into natural contact with peers from other cultures and thus to learn about those cultures indirectly. This is an application of the "contact thesis" developed by Harvard psychologist Gordon Allport (1954). The contact thesis posits that if individuals work together as equals, they will develop bonds of respect and friendship. Slavin (1991) and others have applied this theory in classrooms composed of students who differed by race, social class, academic achievement, and sex and have found that the theory holds true.

Language Study. Studying a foreign language is another way for students (and teachers) to learn about other cultures. This is true in terms of the cultures of the target language, but it also is true in terms of general language principles. Studying a foreign language helps students become aware of language-bound differences among peoples and cultures.

For example, students who study Spanish will learn that Spanish phrasing is tied to cultural views of personal responsibility:

El avión se fué means "The plane left me."
El plato sé cayó means "The plate dropped from my hand."

The comparable English expressions are, "I missed the plane" and "I dropped the plate." In English the speaker takes responsibility for the action. The Spanish speaker is easier on himself or herself. The object has a will of its own.

Another example is worthwhile. In English, one says, "The clock is running." One cannot say that in Spanish. The comparable expression in Spanish is, "The clock is *walking*." What does this say about a cultural sense of time?

Students need not study a language in depth to benefit. Many teachers can learn how to provide an introduction to a variety of languages that will help students gain a stronger sense of other cultures along with a stronger understanding of the way language and culture are interconnected.

Direct Communication. Helping students to connect one-on-one with other students can make for rewarding cross-cultural interactions. A strategy that springs immediately to mind is the setting up of penpal exchanges. Students can find penpals in their own country or other countries and have done so for many years. A new twist is using the Internet for such exchanges.

Electronic penpal exchanges can be facilitated using a variety of online services, such as America Online (AOL), CompuServe, Prodigy, and the Microsoft Network (MSN). Following are several examples of cross-cultural projects that use Internet communication:

- *Winnipeg, Manitoba, and Saco, Maine.* Fourth-grade language arts students in these two cities developed a project called, "Bridging the Gap: Dispelling the American/Canadian Myth," which covered several subjects, including geography, history, and contemporary lifestyles.
- *Quebec and Maine.* Students in schools in Canada and the United States started a project to help the Quebec students learn English and the Maine students learn French. When the Maine students took a field trip to actually meet their Canadian penpals, they were surprised to find that the Quebec students were all profoundly deaf. Signing was their first language, French their second, and English their third.
- *San Francisco and New York.* Schools in these two cities shared information about each other's Spanish/English bilingual program. The San Francisco students were surprised

to learn that their New York counterparts were of African descent but from the Caribbean and thus identified with Hispanic culture. The project also did much to dispel tension in the San Francisco school between African-American and Hispanic students.

- *Global.* High school students in the Americas, Israel, Russia, China, and parts of Europe engaged in a project to gather data and other information about the Holocaust. Many students contacted Holocaust survivors using electronic technology. Another project, the "Nicaragua Rope Pump Project," connected Nicaraguan students with their counterparts around the world. The students shared stories about daily life. When students in Nicaragua mentioned that they must walk four kilometers each day to get water for their homes, the worldwide student network responded by raising more than $10,000 to drill wells and install water pumps closer to the students' homes.

Summary

I started this chapter with the old saying: If you give a man a fish, he will eat for a day; but if you teach a man to fish, he will never go hungry. Empowering students to learn about their own culture and other cultures and to exchange ideas across cultures are strategies for teaching for diversity in a manner that helps students become culturally viable.

I have tried to demonstrate that teachers have wide latitude in designing strategies that accommodate diversity. However, some necessary preconditions are worth reiterating. First, teachers must take into account safety and equality issues. Schools must be places where students feel safe — physically, intellectually, and emotionally. And equality is more than just access; students need the tools to benefit equally from the education offered to them.

Second, instructional strategies that accommodate diversity must be grounded in sound theory. I mentioned Dewey and

Freire, but numerous other theorists, researchers, and practitioners have offered bases for thinking about multiculturalism and how best to help students discover, first, who they are individually and culturally and, then, to help students connect with individuals from other cultures. I have suggested that the teacher's role is less that of the "sage on the stage" and more that of a "guide on the side." The transition from knowledge-giver to learning-enabler may be difficult for some teachers to accept and even harder to implement, but it is essential if students are to be empowered to become their own best teacher and to adopt life-long learning as a personal goal.

Third, facilitative teaching must be seriously taken up, understanding that such teaching is not one-dimensional. Facilitative teaching includes both convergent and divergent strategies. I sketched three areas for special attention by the facilitative teacher: behavior management, critical thinking (including reflective thinking), and cross-cultural interactions.

I have not attempted to create a "cookbook" of strategies in this chapter. Rather, I have tried to suggest broad strategic instructional ideas that will help teachers to examine their teaching methods and to design strategies that will work best for them and their students.

In the next chapter I take up curriculum that reflects diversity. Some critics might suggest that knowing what to teach (curriculum) ought to come before a discussion of how to teach (instruction). I disagree. This chapter on instruction articulates strategic principles, not the process of conveying specific content. Delineating specific content too narrowly is, in fact, more suited to a knowledge-giver philosophy than to a learning-enabler one. But, as I will demonstrate in the chapter that follows, there also are curricular principles that must be examined in effective teaching for diversity.

Chapter Four

DEVELOPING CURRICULA THAT REFLECT DIVERSITY

In *We Fed Them Cactus*, Fabiola Cabeza de Baca wrote:

> We opened the morning and afternoon sessions by singing and the children loved it. The Spanish children knew folk songs and the Anglos, cowboy ballads and hillbilly songs. As a reward for good lessons, we sang these, but I also taught them the songs which are sung in school nowadays. *The Star-Spangled Banner* resounded on the Mesa Rica each school morning. (1954, p. 56)

A hundred years ago Fabiola Cabeza de Baca commenced her teaching career in a one-room country school in the northeastern *llanos* (plains) of New Mexico. She was painfully aware of her limitations. Although her background in Spanish was strong, she knew little about the backgrounds of either the Anglo or the Indian children. She would learn about them by boarding in their homes. She also was painfully aware of the limitations of her curricular materials. The American history book focused on Colonial America, limited to New England. And even that history was sketchy. It did not mention the French or English presence in nearby Canada, for example. It used only one sentence to include

Native Americans — that they helped the Pilgrims celebrate Thanksgiving — and only one sentence nodded to the Hispanic presence in the faraway Southwest.

Undaunted by these limitations, Cabeza de Baca developed her own curriculum in order to equip her students to live in the 20th century. A century later, teachers in today's schools are facing a similar situation. They must, in many cases, devise their own curricula that reflect the diversity that must be recognized in order to live and work in the 21st century.

In this chapter I will examine curricular factors that educators must take into account as they develop curricula that reflect diversity, including the construction of knowledge both individually and socially. I will devote considerable attention to literacy, in particular the development of cultural literacy. And I will suggest guidelines for developing curricular materials, including student-generated materials. My guiding principles in this chapter are 1) to help students increase their self-respect and respect for the views and rights of others and 2) to help teachers choose or create curricula and accompanying instructional materials that exemplify diversity in content and viewpoint.

Construction of Knowledge

Humans learn best by doing and then interpreting what they have done. "Doing" in this instance includes reading and observing, which usually are regarded as passive. In fact, they often are ways of quietly acting, unobtrusively "doing."

James A. Banks (1996) suggests that individuals' sources of knowledge are all around them. Human knowledge is informed by people, events, and physical surroundings. Individuals construct knowledge in an expanding spiral. At the core of this spiral is the subjective, personal level, and the spiral expands outward to the impersonal and remote.

How an individual constructs knowledge becomes that person's *schema*. A schema is a way of viewing the world. Thus each individual also creates a personal worldview, an existential construct that integrates experiences with people, events, emotions, and so on.

A child's worldview begins with a tight focus: first on mother, then on father and other close family and the child's immediate surroundings. Gradually, as the toddler grows, the world outdoors and playmates enter the child's worldview. The child's schema adjusts to incorporate new input. And the spiral continues outward.

Childhood today is very different from in years past, and a child's worldview is broadened by diverse input early on. In Cabeza de Baca's day, students might have had little knowledge beyond their family and the small rural community in which they dwelt. In those days, communication and transportation were unsophisticated. Radios and automobiles were just beginning to be used. Air travel and television had yet to be invented. Today's world comes into the home almost unbidden. Television and video bombard most children daily. And a day's horse-and-wagon trip to a different community, a rare undertaking for many children in 1900, has now been reduced to a few hours by car and is a common occurrence.

Twentieth-century communication and transportation have ensured that the worldviews of today's children are considerably broader and more diverse than those of the children in Cabeza de Baca's school room. In very real ways a child's world was much smaller in Cabeza de Baca's time than it is today. The challenge for educators facing the 21st century is to help their students make sense of — that is, develop schemata to understand — a greatly enlarged world.

Much of the development of an individual worldview — and an individual schema — takes place in social contexts, such as the family, the community, the church, or the school. Humans interact in social groups wherein common experiences form similar worldviews. Group interaction also creates and perpetuates collective memories, which become customs, traditions, legends, folkways, and histories. In these ways individual identity is, to an extent, shaped by group identity. (Group identity also may be shaped or influenced by strong individuals.) Thus social construction of knowledge and personal construction of knowledge are inextricably interwoven.

Social contexts often are also cultural contexts. Families, communities, churches, and even schools may have strongly cohesive cultural identities. But the time when a Greek family might live in a Greek community, attend a Greek church, and associate only with other Greeks has largely passed; and the same is true for most other linguistic, racial, and ethnic groups. While strong cultural identity remains, diversity is the rule in actual contact, whether in the community, the church, or the school. Even in communities that would shut out the diverse world "outside" — think of the Amish or the Hasidim — modern communications media and transportation have made such isolation virtually impossible to sustain. And so the challenge of developing curricula is to incorporate such diversity while simultaneously responding to the cultural identity needs of individuals.

Cultural Literacy

I use the term *cultural literacy* in the same sense as "computer literacy" or "mathematical literacy" — that is, to mean learning about one's own culture and other cultures, to understand the nature and ramifications of "culture." This literacy is distinct from what may be termed functional literacy and critical literacy, though all three have points of linkage. Let me define these terms before going further with cultural literacy.

Functional literacy refers to the ability to speak, understand, read, and write one's native language or, in practical terms, the dominant language of the society in which one lives. For most of the United States and Canada that language is English, though French is the language of currency in Quebec and Spanish is nearly essential in parts of the U.S. Southwest. Functional literacy is the foundation for other forms of literacy, including computer literacy and mathematical literacy, which also require a firm knowledge of the language used to express computer and mathematical concepts.

Critical literacy refers to the ability to think critically and creatively and is the highest (most intellectually sophisticated) form of literacy. To be critically literate means to be able to analyze, synthesize, and evaluate information of many types (literary, historical, scientific, mathematical) and from various sources (reading, observation, research). Individuals who are critically literate are able to make inferences, draw conclusions, generalize, predict outcomes, and engage in other aspects of critical and creative thinking, as I discussed in Chapter Three.

Cultural literacy stands on the base of functional literacy but is most meaningful when critical literacy also is present. While a certain amount of cultural literacy can be gained intuitively, that intuitive knowledge is refined through functional literacy — for example, by reading and listening to cultural information — and is further enhanced and enlarged through critical literacy, or thinking critically and creatively about cultural information.

The pertinent question in attaining cultural literacy is, Which culture? Three intellectual camps predominate in ethnocentric arguments over this question. Should cultural literacy be Eurocentric, Afrocentric, or multicultural? Each of these camps merits a short exploration.

Eurocentric cultural literacy is based on a belief that in Western civilization the traditions and cultures of Europe should be regarded as cultural exemplars. Knowledge of greatest worth, Eurocentric tradition goes, is derived from the European cultures and their roots in Ancient Greece and Rome. For example, when one thinks of Great Literature, one should turn to Shakespeare, Milton, Dante, Aristotle, Plato, and so on — the great writers of Western civilization. Thus, for the Eurocentrists, the best curriculum is one that draws from this European heritage.

Afrocentric cultural literacy is based on a belief that Western culture, in fact, has strong roots in African cultures. Ancient Greece was indebted to Africa for much of its development. Furthermore, modern North American culture also is much indebted to African influences by way of the slave trade, which brought not just strong hands and backs but also strong traditions

91

of history, language, music, and art. Afrocentrism is not simply an African-American reaction to the predominance of Eurocentrism; it is an ethnocentrism that adherents believe harkens to a deeper cultural history.

Multiculturalism is, in a sense, a middle ground. The multiculturalist's view is that Western civilization can be linked solely with neither the European cultural history nor its supposedly deeper roots in African cultures. Rather, multiculturalism posits that North American culture, as a whole, is a culture of pluralism and diversity — in fact, many cultures. These cultures retain distinct identities even as their members work toward common values, beliefs, and goals in order to nourish a cohesive unity: "American" society or "Canadian" society.

Moreover, the concept of culture under the rubric of multiculturalism is broader than ethnic, racial, linguistic, or national heritage. Culture also includes a variety of other factors by which humans form collectivities or communities, however loosely knit. Such factors include family, sex, sexual orientation, gender, economic status (or class), ability or disability, and so on. In other words, every aspect of diversity also is an aspect of culture.

A multicultural view of cultural literacy, then, is that such knowledge should focus on the construction of meaning based on multiple perspectives: one's own culture, the culture of the society at hand, and the global culture as expressed through common concerns and values. Ralph Waldo Emerson, the American essayist, said that each generation must write its own books and find its own solutions to problems. Each individual must define his or her own multifaceted culture.

Curricula for Cultural Literacy

I have purposely used the plural *curricula* in the chapter title, because there is no one best curriculum for developing cultural literacy or for reflecting diversity. In place of a canon there must be an attitude, informed by many perspectives and grounded in a thorough understanding of instructional strategies. Indeed, I would argue that the instructional process is, to some degree, the curriculum. Developing cultural literacy is more about process than product. I resist both the holistic (the curriculum is what is taught), as too general, and the codified (the curriculum is what school authorities mandate to be taught), as too restrictive. Between these extremes lies a true middle ground, which is what I propose to outline in this section.

As a course of study, a curriculum can be compared to a play. Teachers (and administrators, to some extent) are the playwrights and directors; students are the actors. In true-life theatrical productions, the playwrights and directors construct the play by drawing not merely on the ideas they want to express but also on the actors' capabilities, backgrounds, and interests. Likewise, the actors do not merely mouth the playwright's words or march through the director's staging. They also bring to bear their views of the plot, their understanding of the characters, and so on. In other words, teachers and students — playwrights, directors, and actors — work together to construct the curriculum, to create meaningful learning — to stage the play.

For discussion purposes it is perhaps easiest to think of the lesson unit as a building block for constructing curricula. Again, the plural is intentional, because such units may be linked or collected in various ways to create quite different curricula, depending on the needs and interests of teachers and students and the constraints of state or school district mandates, available funds and facilities, and other factors. A lesson unit must include certain basic features:

- A set of questions or statements (generalizations) that frame the unit topic.
- Key concepts and terms related to the main idea to be examined in the unit.
- Objectives that specify what students should know or be able to do as a result of the unit.
- An assessment plan that includes: 1) activating students' prior knowledge (finding out what students know in advance

of study), 2) ongoing assessment that allows for redirection or recapitulation, and 3) final assessment (finding out what students have learned as a result of the unit).

- A projection of how the unit content will affect the student in non-cognitive ways; understanding the unit's psychomotor and affective potential.
- Sequential challenges designed to lead students to do more complex, higher-level thinking over the course of the unit.
- A list of resources needed to effectively implement the unit.

This list of basic features is fairly standard in curriculum planning, perhaps with the exception of projecting psychomotor and affective content potential. In teaching for diversity, however, that item is quite important. It relates to students' ability to respond to instruction. I will illustrate this concern by suggesting several potential unit topics that can be useful in the development of cultural literacy. These suggested topics are necessarily broad; the specific treatment of the topic will depend on the maturity of the students and the context into which the unit is to fit. However, each topic is a diversity factor around which many different units and lessons within units might be developed.

Ability. There is great diversity in human abilities. Scientists are discovering new information about human abilities almost daily, or so it seems. For example, rather than speaking of intelligence as a general cognitive attribute, scientists are now speaking of multiple forms of intelligence. Students might explore Howard Gardner's concept of multiple intelligences and evaluate their own intelligences. Another example of diversity in human abilities is the physical dimension and how society responds to individuals that it labels "disabled" or "handicapped." How have societies in the past treated individuals with disabilities, and how are such persons treated today?

Class. While democracies such as the United States and Canada strive to be "classless" societies, socioeconomic class distinctions are plain. Many critics see the nature of work changing in the information age, and the middle class seems to be shrinking. For many students, being poor and at risk are paired conditions. One problem that students might examine is cultural discontinuity: What cultural challenges do students from impoverished backgrounds face when they come to school and are confronted by teachers whose backgrounds are overwhelmingly middle class.

Ethnicity. Everyone has an ethnic background, but many students are unaware of theirs. In particular, white students of European descent often have no personal means of relating to the ethnic concerns expressed by Hispanic, black, or Asian students. One way to help such students understand ethnic concerns is to encourage them to find their own ethnic roots through personal history, autobiography, or genealogy.

Race. As immigrant nations, both Canada and the United States are race conscious. Racial differences also ripple through other manifestations of diversity, such as overrepresentation of blacks in that segment of the population below the poverty line. Students might ponder whether some differences in attitudes toward ethnicity or gender roles also are differentiated according to race. And what about mixed-racial heritages? These diversity topics also can help students understand themselves and others.

Religion. What role does religion play in values development? How are students' notions of right and wrong determined: by basic morality, by religious teaching, and so on? How does religion interact with race, class, ethnicity, and gender? While the doctrine of church-state separation prohibits the teaching of religion, it does not discourage the consideration of religion as a factor of diversity. And, at least for some students, religion plays an important role in their lives.

Sex and Gender. Diversity also includes differences of sex and gender roles. Apart from obvious physical differences, how do males and females differ — for example, in their sense of self and others? How are males and females differentiated by gender roles, and how does society assign those roles? For children and adolescents, these are compelling topics of interest. Exploring such diversity can help students develop a better sense of their potential and can build self-esteem.

Sexual Orientation. Related to sex and gender issues, the issue of sexual orientation is one that educators (and parents) shy away from. Indeed, schools tend to discourage any discussion of sexual matters, often to the detriment of students who have burning questions that need to be answered. By age 12 most students are discovering their sexuality, and one issue in this process of discovery is sexual orientation. Pertinent, non-threatening discussions of homosexual and heterosexual issues can help students to successfully negotiate the often turbulent sexual waters of adolescence.

Family. A student's family life plays a key factor in the student's development of self-esteem and the values he or she brings to school. A declining percentage of students comes from the stereotypical "traditional" family, and so an exploration of family diversity can be productive. This topic should include blended families, adoptive families, single-parent families, mixed-race families, families headed by gay or lesbian parents, and families headed by someone other than a student's parent, such as a grandparent or other relative or a foster parent.

Four Approaches to Teaching for Cultural Literacy

Banks (1989) suggests four approaches to teaching about diverse people: a contributions approach, an additive approach, a transformative approach, and a decision-making and social action approach. Taken in this order, these approaches also represent a hierarchy for infusing diverse cultural content into a curriculum. How these approaches are conceived and implemented will be guided by the students' levels of prior knowledge and their maturity.

A Contributions Approach. At the most basic level a curriculum can be designed to include diverse cultural elements. This does not mean merely a simplistic "heroes and holidays" contribution, however. A contributions approach may include the use of guest speakers who represent various cultures; reading books, stories, and articles about various cultures; attending cultural events, such as a Cinco de Mayo celebration; and so on. Outside the humanities, in which most of the work on cultural literacy is done, a contributions approach also can open new pathways to knowledge. In science, for example, students might investigate non-traditional medicines and medical treatments, such as the use of herbal remedies by Native Americans or Chinese acupuncture.

The greatest drawback of a contributions approach is its superficiality. This approach touches the surface features of diverse cultures, but it does not go below that surface. For example, the contributions approach might permit students to learn about the use of herbal medicine but probably would not delve into Native American values and beliefs that undergird such use. Another potential problem of this approach is that it may inadvertently reinforce cultural stereotypes, particularly if it treats cultural elements as once-a-year curiosities.

An Additive Approach. The step above a contributions approach is an additive approach. To carry the previous example further, an additive approach would delve into the Native American values and beliefs about herbal medicine. And such information would be integrated into the regular curriculum, rather than treated as a curiosity. To contrast these two approaches further: Noting the Indian presence in the Thanksgiving celebration is indicative of a contributions approach; examining that contribution and the pervasive contributions of Native Americans to the early formation of Colonial America would exemplify an additive approach.

Other examples of an additive approach are learning about the contributions of Chinese laborers in the building of the first railroads and how that endeavor affected the Chinese culture of that period or considering versions of familiar stories, such as *Yeh Shen* (Ai-Ling 1982) and *Mufaro's Beautiful Daughters* (Steptoe 1987), both retellings of the Cinderella story, and comparing and contrasting how those versions differ from one another along cultural lines.

The disadvantage of an additive approach is that it is still rather superficial, even though cultural information is better integrated into the curriculum than in a contributions approach. There is still a risk of reinforcing stereotypes, rather than dispelling them; and there is little linkage to the students themselves — their lives, their histories, their futures.

A Transformative Approach. Unlike the first two approaches, a transformative approach is intended to change the basic curriculum, not just add to it. Both the contributions approach and the additive approach treat cultural information like the chrome on an automobile, an enhancement, attractive but not essential. A transformative approach tinkers with the engine. Let me illustrate this approach with an example.

Take North American history. Study usually begins with the first European immigrants to the New World. This is a Eurocentric approach. A transformative approach would recognize that North American history starts much earlier, say, with the theory that Asian peoples migrating across the Bering Strait centuries before became the first Native Americans. Or, if that is too far back in history, then an alternative might be to consider the status of Indian tribes — how and where they lived, the various affinity groups, contested lands, and so on — just prior to the coming of European settlers. Then students also might explore how the Native Americans viewed the Europeans' arrival, the role played by various tribes and individuals responding to the European immigration, and so on.

One of the criticisms of Eurocentric history is that the viewpoints of nondominant participants often are missing. A transformative approach attempts to correct this problem by introducing those missing elements. The key is balance — in other words, *not* rewriting history from the opposite perspective but, on the contrary, rewriting history to include all perspectives. The same is true for the inclusion of other cultural elements, such as literature from other cultures. Such literature is not intended to replace but to complement.

A Decision-Making and Social Action Approach. This approach takes the transformative approach a step further. This approach not only is intended to change the basic curriculum, it also is intended to help students think for themselves — that is, to make decisions based on knowledge constructed and to take responsible social action based on those decisions. To carry the previous example forward a step, students might do research to find out about human migration in North America, both before and after the influx of Europeans. They might compare and contrast historical accounts across cultures, and from such an investigation they also might think critically about ethical issues related to conquest and domination. Or they might turn to creative thinking and develop stories, artworks, or drama to depict early North American history and culture.

This approach focuses on higher-order thinking skills: analysis, synthesis, and evaluation. Students analyze cultural information, taking a proactive approach to gathering such information, rather than receiving it passively. They bring together diverse information and construct new knowledge by adding to and modifying their prior understandings. And they evaluate knowledge, deciding what is most worth knowing and determining actions based on such evaluation. It is through the decision-making and social action approach that students can best be prepared to debunk stereotypes and combat biases with regard to race, socioeconomic status, ethnicity, sex, sexual orientation, and the like.

The development of cultural literacy is a lifelong process. Banks' hierarchy of approaches is helpful in framing that learning process, not merely for students but also for teachers and parents. The hierarchy may be practically applied as teachers plan curricula to ensure that cultural content goes beyond the superficial.

Choosing Curricular Materials

For most of this chapter I have focused on the conceptual construction of curricula: sources of knowledge, cultural contexts, and particularly the development of cultural literacy. I touched on creating cultural literacy curricula, giving special attention to the construction of study units and suggesting possible topics related to diversity. Then I introduced Banks' hierarchy of approaches to cultural literacy instruction as a way of thinking about curricular content. Next, I will zero in on choosing curricular materials. My purpose here is get below the surface and to dig deep into Banks' decision-making and social action approach. In other words, I want to try to answer the question: What materials will best transform the curriculum and actively involve students in directing their own learning?

Teaching about diverse cultures demands that teachers give careful attention to the selection of curricular materials. This is nothing new. Many commercially prepared materials treat culture superficially, and much of the information is inaccurate or incomplete. That is true in other fields as well. But those who would teach about culture must be particularly on the lookout for cultural biases, stereotypes, and misrepresentations.

Another perspective is inclusivity. It is all too easy to approach a topic with blinders on. Too narrow a focus can exclude diversity. For example, in teaching a unit on World War II one curricular focus might be on the strategies used by the winning generals. While this approach will provide one perspective on how the Allies succeeded in winning the war, it also will neglect much of the real work of the soldiers under those generals, such as crack fighting units of African Americans and Native Americans, and women, whose work both in and out of uniform was an essential element of the Allied success. My point is that World War II is an enormous topic. It is legitimate to narrow the topic. But in so narrowing, it also is important to ensure that the topic remains broad enough to admit diversity.

Another way of approaching the diversity issue is to focus on various cultures individually in a series of units, rather than attempting to look at many cultural elements in a single unit. While this approach is not appropriate in every discipline, it can be used effectively in many humanities contexts. This type of approach comes under the rubric of ethnic studies. The ethnic studies model that I will detail in the next few paragraphs grew out of the "intergroup education" movement of the 1950s. That movement was an attempt to offer students experiences to reduce racial prejudice and, indeed, emphasized experience in general over acquisition of book knowledge.

The ethnic studies model operates with the following features:

- Goal: To foster increased knowledge and understanding of a cultural group.
- Operational assumption: Increased cultural knowledge will lead to better understanding and acceptance or tolerance of difference.
- Conceptual frame: Study is based on beliefs that the cultural group is: 1) dynamic and in the process of growth and change, 2) organized by a system of beliefs and values, 3) internally diverse, and 4) both similar to and different from other cultural groups.

With this operational definition in mind, the ethnic studies model might be tailored by a disciplinary focus. For example, rather than investigating all aspects of a cultural group, students in a writing class might focus on literature produced by writers in the culture under study, or students in a history class might focus on one culture's interactions with another over the course of time.

Let me now tie the use of the ethnic studies model to the selection of curricular materials. Certain principles merit application. The principles that follow also can be generalized to apply to materials selection in many other contexts, in addition to the ethnic studies model.

Multiple Perspectives. Curricular materials need to include both internal and external perspectives, or how those inside the culture view themselves as well as how those outside the culture view them. One might consider these viewpoints as autobiographical and biographical. But a note of caution: They cannot be considered subjective (insider) and objective (outsider). This would be merely the elitism of the external observer. In fact, the observer/outsider viewpoint may be as subjective as the insider viewpoint.

A few examples may be useful. Yankton Sioux Joseph Iron Eye Dudley's *Choteau Creek* (1992) and Hopi Polingaysi

Qoyawayma's *No Turning Back* (1964) are examples of insider perspectives. They offer a cultural analysis from the viewpoint of someone in the culture of study. But it also would be well to remember that such a viewpoint is personal as well as cultural. Dudley cannot speak for all of the Yankton Sioux; Qoyawayma cannot speak for all of the Hopi. On the other hand, Ruth Benedict's classic, *Patterns of Culture* (1934), is an example of an outsider perspective. Benedict describes seven Native American tribes and their cultures, based on ethnographic research done by several anthropologists. But, while the writing is accurate in its descriptions, Benedict's viewpoint is informed by her own cultural sensibilities, not by the sensibilities of her subjects.

These examples, both insider and outsider, are essentially *looking into* the culture. Dudley and Qoyawayma are examples of introspection. In some cases it can be useful to understand how a culture *looks out* at the rest of the world or at another culture. When I was studying the colonization of New Mexico by Spain (1598-1691), I read original documents and secondary accounts told from the perspective of the Hispanic settlers. I came away with the idea that New Mexico offered the Hispanic colonists many advantages, such as ample free land on which to graze sheep and cattle. Later, I came upon some accounts that offered the perspective of the Pueblo people, the Native Americans in that region. They saw the Hispanic "invaders" quite differently. From this reading I discovered that the Hispanic settler's "advantages" were hard won. In fact, the early Hispanic colonists brought diseases and slavery, both of which decimated the Pueblo people, who expelled the colonists for a time. When the Hispanic settlers returned, they did away with slavery and began to intermarry with the Pueblo people. Only through developing family and economic ties, then, did the Hispanic settlers achieve the advantages they found in the new land. I would not have gained this fuller picture had I not stumbled on the Pueblo perspective, looking not at themselves but at the Hispanic settlers. Along with the Hispanic accounts, these Pueblo accounts gave me a more complete sense of the culture of that place and time.

Multiple perspectives, using both insider and outsider views, help to ensure that students analyze viewpoints, find threads of commonality and differences in cultural values and beliefs, and draw their own conclusions about the "objective" nature of the culture under study.

Culture as Dynamic. Living cultures are ever-changing. Curricular materials need to portray this factor. Too often students are exposed only to a snapshot of a culture, and it may be a stereotypical view at that. For example, when elementary textbooks include information on foreign cultures, they often portray traditional folkways and traditional dress. Students gain a misimpression that such things are the norm when, in fact, traditional dress, for example, may be worn only on ceremonial occasions.

If culture is reduced to "snapshots," then at least there must be many such snapshots, so that the composite forms a more complete picture of the culture. Cross-cultural contact and the import and export of cultural ideas and products mean that all cultures are dynamic, rather than static. This dynamic must be visible for study.

An example of this dynamic is the introduction of the rodeo to the American West. When Anglo cowboys first came into contact with Mexican cowboys in the early 1800s, they noticed that the Mexicans played games while waiting for straggling cattle to be rounded up. The games included calf-roping and bullriding, which they carried on during the roundup, or in Spanish, *rodear*. The Anglo cowboys joined in the fun, calling the activities by their version of *rodear*: rodeo. Over time, rodeos became a regular fixture of the Western cattle drive and eventually were transformed into the entertainments that still occur today. Thus the American cowboy culture was changed by contact with the Mexican cowboy culture.

Cross-pollination of cultures occurs through contacts that may be made in person or through some form of communication, such as reading books. Twentieth century transportation and communication advances have made cross-cultural contacts more frequent and more extensive. In past centuries an idea might circle the globe over a course of years; now it takes only seconds. Curricular materials for teaching about cultures need to recognize this dynamic.

Values and Beliefs. Curricular materials need to portray a culture's basic values and the beliefs that undergird them. Cultural practices do not arise from air; they have bases in belief. Therefore, if students are to understand a culture well, they must be able to examine the culture's beliefs.

For example, students might examine the beliefs that undergird the Japanese value of group identity. Those beliefs might be set against the American beliefs that undergird the "rugged individual" value observed in the United States. This topic might be pursued through a study of short stories from both countries, by looking at each nation's economic policies and practices, or by probing the historical events leading up to the Second World War as carried on in the Pacific. Such examination of cultural values and beliefs can be tied to a number of different subjects or disciplines.

Conflicting beliefs often give rise to prejudice and persecution. Thus gaining an understanding of other cultures' beliefs can be a first step in combating the destructiveness of cultural prejudices, such as racism, sexism, or homophobia.

Intragroup Diversity. Curricular materials also need to go beyond the monolithic. Stereotypes portray individuals within a culture as all alike. This is never the reality. No matter how cohesive the group, however commonly held their beliefs, every group is composed of individuals.

Failure to recognize intragroup diversity is endemic to "snapshot" curricula. Students need opportunities not just to learn about the common features of a culture but also to study the exceptions. "Blacks came to America as slaves" is a snapshot example. Yes, many black people did come to America as slaves, but others came of their own free will. Absolutes are seldom accurate.

While it may be politically expedient to speak of groups as monoliths — the Jewish experience, the black perspective, the

Hispanic attitude — such descriptions are rarely entirely true. There is great diversity among the experiences of Jews; African-Americans hold many viewpoints; and attitudes among Hispanic individuals are as divergent as among the general population. Curricular materials need to make such intragroup diversity plain in order to dispel misleading images — in short, to characterize, rather than caricature.

Intergroup Similarity. This principle is the counterpart of intragroup diversity. Curricular materials need to examine similarities among cultural groups, not just differences. Too often information provided to students points up only how "The Other" is different from them. In fact, many cultural groups have similar beliefs, values, customs, literature, and practices. I provided an example earlier when I suggested comparing and contrasting various cultures' versions of the Cinderella story. Even very young students can profit from this kind of activity.

Moreover, understanding cross-cultural similarities can be another way to overcome stereotypes and prejudices. Humans tend to demonize those whom they see as "different." Therefore, to engender a sense of the totality of humanity, it is important for students to see those from other cultures as, in many ways, like themselves.

These broad principles articulate a way of approaching ethnic studies and teaching for diversity in general. Following is a series of subject-based questions that might be used to start students thinking about diversity. These are merely examples:

- *History.* How do cultures, such as ethnic groups, transmit their beliefs and values? Can a relationship be drawn between storytelling and collective memory?
- *Science.* There is one human race but many racial variations. How do skin color, body type, and other physical differences work as racial markers?
- *Mathematics.* While mathematics has many universals, it also can be culture-bound. Consider mathematical notation and how math is used in other cultures.

- *Geography.* How does migration affect culture? When cultures collide, what happens?
- *Economics.* How do culture and economics interact? Consider the Plains Indians' use of the buffalo before and after the coming of white settlers.
- *Literature.* Cultures are reflected in their literature, and cultural beliefs are the basis for a culture's myths. What do tribal myths say about the beliefs of various Native American cultures.
- *Language.* When two cultures communicate, both are likely changed. How has English affected the French language, and vice versa?
- *Visual Arts.* How are the arts of a culture changed by contact with other cultures? Examine so-called folk art, or naive art, for indications of cross-cultural influences.
- *Performing Arts.* Music, dance, and drama tell the stories of a culture. How are a culture's performances changed through cross-cultural communication?

Teachers and students can extend these sample questions and develop new questions along many lines of inquiry. To these principles and examples I would add only three admonitions:

- Treat cultural expressions with respect. Avoid cultural elitism, such as labeling one expression "high culture" and another "low culture." Such elitism also extends to judgments about validity, such as characterizing a single-parent home as a "broken home." Many two-parent homes are "broken," or dysfunctional; and many single-parent homes are healthy and vital.
- Celebrate cultures in context. The "heroes and holidays" approach is limiting; deeper digging into cultures reveals a richer reality. But cultural holidays and events should be celebrated. It is appropriate to celebrate the memory of Martin Luther King Jr. on the memorial holiday in January; but it is inappropriate then to ignore African-American issues and culture during the rest of the year.

- Look for the ordinary as well as the extraordinary. Cultures are milieus of residence. Students need to see the everyday aspects of a culture as well as its holidays and festivals.

Student-Created Curricula

Finally, a point that I have already emphasized is getting students to invest in their own learning. Curricula, including materials, generated by students themselves have a powerful immediacy and relevance.

I began this chapter with a quote from Fabiola Cabeza de Baca's book, the spirit of which bears reiteration: Students should be encouraged to bring their cultures to school. While the old melting-pot view was to encourage students to leave their cultures outside the schoolhouse door in order to be free to embrace a new culture within, teaching for diversity means encouraging students to do precisely the opposite. By bringing their cultures into the classroom, students can help to enhance their own understandings (through introspection) and to enlarge their teachers' and their peers' knowledge of their cultures.

When teachers help students to formalize a curriculum and to create or select curricular materials to support and extend learning, they also are teaching important skills. For example, they can help students to develop a sense of voice and audience and to understand the power of language (Au 1993). When students see and hear others responding to their curriculum, they realize that they can influence how others create knowledge and build understanding.

The making of curricula need not be confined to older students. Kathryn Au (1993) describes several student-developed curricula that involve very young students. For example, kindergartners in a Seattle school planned and created a 10-minute video and six small books to show younger children what it would be like to enter kindergarten. The materials covered such topics as the school bus, recess, and lunch and sought to quell fears that newcomers might have about coming to kindergarten. The kinder-

107

gartners were explaining the school culture to those who would follow them into it.

Other examples of curricula and materials that even quite young students can develop include:

- visual displays, dioramas, bulletin boards;
- electronic or computer-generated visuals, including web sites;
- research projects and reports;
- panel discussions, debates, and forums;
- articles for school and local newspapers;
- stories for telling and reading, skits, scripts; and
- family histories, biographies, autobiographies.

As students develop curricula and supporting materials, teachers also can encourage students to follow the same kinds of steps that they follow: identifying purposes, defining objectives, structuring activities, selecting materials, choosing assessment strategies, and so on.

Fabiola Cabeza de Baca, whose Spanish- and English-speaking children brought their cultures to school in songs and stories, was on the right track. All students should be encouraged to take pride in their cultural heritage and to share that pride and knowledge with others as they also learn about different cultures. The experience of Cabeza de Baca reifies what Banks, Au, and others have pointed out, that students' sources of knowledge are all around them. When teachers help and encourage students to bring their cultures into the classroom, they enrich the environment for all students and make teaching for diversity a reality.

But what about the next step? How can educators teach students to live in a diverse society, the society outside the schoolhouse door? Teaching for diversity is one thing within the smaller microenvironment of the school and classroom. Is it a different thing in the macro-environment of the "real world"? That is the question I will take up in Chapter Five.

Chapter Five

TEACHING STUDENTS TO LIVE IN A DIVERSE SOCIETY

In *Democracy and Social Ethics*, turn-of-the-century social reformer and Nobel Peace Prize winner Jane Addams wrote:

> The democratic ideal demands of the school that it shall give the child's own experience a social value; that it shall teach him to direct his activities and adjust them to those of other people. (1907, p. 180)

Bringing up children to live successfully beyond the family and the school has always been a shared responsibility. That is common across all cultures. The cliché is true: It does take a whole village to raise a child.

In this chapter I will focus on socialization, teaching students to live in a diverse society, which I suggest is an outgrowth of school activities that foster self-respect and teach respect for the views and rights of others. I believe that such activities are best conducted in schools and classrooms that operate from a conviction that they must become communities of learners.

Socialization and Diversity

Socialization is the process of teaching and learning social values. Take kissing, for example. Imagine a second-grade class. During recess Dick chases Jane in a game of kissing tag. "Georgie Porgie, puddin' an' pie, kissed the girls and made them cry!" he hollers. Jane runs away, giggling. When Dick catches her, he plants a kiss on her cheek and yells, "Gotcha!"

Another second-grader, Susie, wants Bill to be her boyfriend. After lunchtime play they are hanging up their coats. Alone in the hallway for a moment, Susie slips up behind Bill, spins him around, and quickly kisses his cheek. Bill objects and later complains to his mother, who calls the teacher.

At recess Jean trips over a jump rope and falls down, skinning one knee. Tony, a second-grade classmate, runs over to comfort her. He helps her to her feet, puts his arm awkwardly around her shoulder, and kisses her cheek. "You'll be okay," he says.

Second-grade kisses: Are they all the same? One kiss in play, one of unwelcome affection, one for comforting a hurt. The call from the mother whose son was kissed against his wishes might push more reactionary educators — given recent headlines about alleged sexual harassment in elementary schools — to ban all kisses in second grade. But that would be a legalistic approach, not an educational one.

My point is that teaching social values also means exploring the motivations and reasons behind our actions in various contexts, those contexts being social settings of many different kinds. Blanket rules — no kissing, no wearing your hat when you eat — usually are wrong, or at least confusing to students, regardless of their age. Yes, it may be inappropriate to wear your hat at the dinner table or in a nice restaurant, but what about when you are eating a hot dog at a baseball game? A kiss of innocent comfort *is* different from an unwanted expression of affection. It is those differences that educators must elucidate and that students must learn or, in many cases, discover for themselves — but hopefully within a supportive environment.

Teaching for diversity treads a similarly precarious line. Because communities are becoming increasingly diverse, the community-as-teacher or village-as-child-rearer metaphor needs the help of formalized socialization, which is the province of schools. Canadian scholar John Friesen in his study, *When Cultures Clash*, comments:

> Canada is a society rife with contradictions. One of the most striking features of our society is the great disparity which exists in its reward structure and the consequent inequalities. (1993, p. 119)

John Davidson Hunter, on the U.S. side of the border, comments similarly in *Culture Wars: The Struggle to Define America*:

> Moral pluralism has expanded and seems to promise to expand further. . . . Traditional sources of an underlying cultural, political, and legal consensus are less and less credible to vast segments of the population. (1991, p. 314)

How, then, can teachers approach this task of socialization? One way that I would suggest is to recreate the concept of "the village" in the classroom. If students learn how to function well in the microcosmic community of the classroom, then they will be more likely to take on those skills and characteristics that will allow them to function well in — that is, to be socialized to — the larger human community beyond the schoolyard.

From Medieval Village to Global Village

The model I will draw on is the open-field village of medieval Europe. The idea of "the village" comes from the Latin term, *communitas villae*, meaning a "community of the villa." A community of this type was organized around the landowner's home, or villa, and made up of workers who, for the most part, farmed the land that lay around the villa in open fields. These small communities of workers became villages. And, if the landowner gained more land or became wealthier, the villa might become a castle or fortress; and the village might grow into a city.

A village community looked after everyone and everything within its province:

> The medieval village. . . was the primary community to which its people belonged for all life's purposes. There they lived, they labored, there they socialized, loved, married . . . had children . . . got sick, died and were buried. (Gies and Gies 1990, p. 7)

If a tree needed felling, the villagers came together to get the job done. If someone's barn burned down, the villagers came together to put up a new one. At the same time, there also were differences among the villagers. Some villagers had claim to more land than others; some had claim to no land at all but lived by other work, such as carpentry or shoemaking. And, while the principal landowner could rightly behave as an autocrat, it often fell to the villagers to govern themselves so that work could be accomplished and disagreements could be resolved peaceably.

The ideal of the medieval village is an apt model for the classroom community. Its best features — absent the autocratic landowner (or autocratic teacher) — suggest the best features of a democratic society. These can be summed up as 1) having a common purpose, 2) maintaining stability, 3) fostering cooperation, and 4) balancing independence and interdependence. Each of these characteristics merits a few words about its application to the classroom community.

Common purpose. To function as a community, any group must have one or more common purposes. The overriding purpose of attending school is to learn — perhaps, more accurately, to learn how to learn. More specific purposes complement this basic purpose, such as to learn how to read or how to speak another language. While some purposes are determined by the teacher (or the administration, or the state, or some other regulatory entity), many of the most meaningful purposes will be determined by the students themselves, either individually or in groups.

Stability. Schools and classrooms function best when students exercise self-control and take appropriate initiative. As students mature, they take on increasing self-governance responsibilities. One purpose of schools is to encourage students to become life-long learners, and to do so will require that students eventually become their own best teachers. Through introspection, students will become adept at determining what they need to know and how best to go about learning it.

Cooperation. Communities are not merely collections of individuals all going about their business unaware of one another. Riders on the same bus do not constitute a community just because they are all together in the same vehicle. In other words, proximity does not equate to community. Rather, community means that students respond to one another, help one another, and take on tasks that draw out individual talents for common ends.

Independence and interdependence. The best communities balance independence ("rugged individualism") with interdependence (cooperation, collaboration), just as Western democracies must achieve such balance in order to function successfully. The watchwords are freedom within order. Students need to learn how to work well with one another and how to determine when a task can best be done alone or with others.

While the medieval village was internally engaged in community-building processes, it was insular as a unit, for the most part functioning independently from other villages. Trade, in many cases, was minimal; and so was communication from village to village, except among those in closest proximity. But the world changed, and the Middle Ages are now long behind us. In spite of that historical distance, the ideal of the medieval village is even more important today than it was in the intervening centuries. Modern communications and information-age commerce have made the community-building processes that took place inside the medieval village essential on a global scale.

Canadian cultural critic and communication theorist Marshall McLuhan coined the phrase, *global village.* He was thinking of a network of people who are linked electronically. He described the global village as a computer-based, satellite and media network (McLuhan and Powers 1989). The emergence of computer technology and satellite television has indeed allowed us to link with strangers in a worldwide web of electronic-based relationships. But there is more to the global village notion than electronics; it also includes what electronic linkages have permitted. For example, such technology also facilitates and speeds economic linkages.

Globalization of national economies also is changing the notion of community, as nations with very different value systems are forced, in order to do business, to seek ways to cooperate. The transnational corporate conglomerate must function, at least to a degree, as a mammoth medieval village — a global village.

As villages were transformed into larger communities, what was once personal and intimate became something else. Urbanization changed the nature of community. Cities became not large villages, but collections of small villages in the form of ethnic neighborhoods and enclaves whose cohesion was built on lines of socioeconomic status, class, language, race, or other factors. For a time the city as a collection of relatively autonomous precincts or neighborhoods preserved the insularity of these individual "villages." However, modern communication and transportation, democratic social initiatives (such as desegregation), the continuing influx of immigrants (which affects both the United States and Canada), and other forces in the new information age have torn down the remaining walls around these villages. We all now live in the same village, the global village. And that is the reality into which students will emerge when they leave the small communities within their schools and classrooms.

Students who are brought up — in school — using the village concept are being socialized to a worldview of a global community. The same best qualities of the medieval village, replicated in the school, are also those that will set the stage for achieving common world purposes, maintaining global stability, cooperating across borders and cultures, and balancing independence (both personal and national) with global interdependence.

Socialization in Action

In Chapter One I suggested that the role of education is to produce "viable" individuals. Viable individuals are capable of sustaining an intellectual life and of growing and developing mentally. I referred to Dewey's dictum: Education is life; life is education. Socialization through the building of a classroom community, a classroom "village," should provide opportunities for students (to paraphrase Jane Addams) to determine the social value of their experiences and activities. Learning how to balance autonomy, self-governance, and social responsibility is a prerequisite for functioning successfully in a democratic society and for becoming a viable individual, a lifelong learner.

A functional model for socialization begins with the school and the teacher, who are collectively responsible for providing a safe environment conducive to learning. Readers may recall that in Chapter Three I sketched a broad definition of "safety," which includes mental as well as physical safety. Students must feel safe to be themselves and to think for themselves, even when their backgrounds, lifestyles, and ideas diverge from the mainstream.

Within the classroom the teacher is the leader — hopefully more democratic than autocratic — who sets the tone and direction of the classroom community, a "village" in which the students will function as interdependent scholars. Together, teacher and students work to balance individual and group concerns. These concerns include: self-interest and the common good, independence and interdependence, and rights and responsibilities (both individual and group). Each of these three balance points merits further discussion.

Self-Interest and the Common Good. Ted, a fifth-grade Native American student, is fascinated by the history of the Sioux, who are important in his heritage. The fifth-grade curriculum requires students to study the opening of the American West, but the standard textbook approaches the subject almost entirely from the white settlers' point of view. How can the teacher and the students balance the requirements of the curriculum with sensitivity to diversity generally and to individual interests, such as Ted's?

One way might be to supplement the textbook with other viewpoints on the opening of the West, including the views of the

Sioux during that period. That could answer the general diversity concern. Another strategy might be to allow students to extend their learning about the opening of the West by choosing individual research projects. Ted might choose to do research about the Sioux, and other students would be free to choose other topics related to the general theme. Such curricular adaptations would serve to balance students' individual interests, which often are expressions of self-interest,* and the common good, which is served by the topic or theme of general study.

Certainly, the teacher might structure an instructional approach to the topic along these lines without involving students in such planning. But how much more valuable for the students it is when they can take part in devising ways to accommodate diversity and individual interests. By involving students in making such decisions, teachers help students learn not just the subject matter at hand but also how to work together, how to address diversity issues, and how to balance self-interest and the common good.

Independence and Interdependence. Free societies operate from a high value placed on independence of the individual. The democracies of Canada and the United States prize self-reliance and individual initiative, but they also must weigh that freedom against the needs of the society as a whole. The freedom of the individual always must be balanced against the good of the community, the nation.

Classroom communities must function as microcosms of the larger community. Students must learn self-reliance and must take initiative, but they also must learn how to work with others, how to compromise and cooperate. For example, four students are expected to work together on an art project, a paper "mural"

---

*I am making a slight distinction here between individual interests and self-interest. Individual interests are those that students articulate on the basis of curiosity, such as an interest in stamp collecting or the history of rifles. Self-interest refers to topics or questions that arise from issues of personal identity and self-esteem, such as Ted's interest in the Sioux because of his Native American heritage.

to be mounted in the hallway. The teacher might initiate this project by discussing with students how the task could be approached. One way, of course, would be simply to mark off four sections on the large paper and let each student work independently. But this strategy would hardly produce a cohesive mural. A better alternative might be to encourage students to talk about their individual strengths.

For example, Matt is very good at drawing human figures. Steve does best with animals, such as horses and dogs. Ellen can handle trees, buildings, and flowers well. And Joan is very good at drawing vehicles, such as cars and trains. By tapping their individual skills and then pooling their resources, the students can produce a mural with many well-drawn elements. This strategy maintains students' independence while also requiring that they plan and work interdependently.

Cooperation of this type is not without precedent. The astute teacher also might seize this "teachable moment" to discuss medieval and early Renaissance artists' schools and studios, in which several artisans would work under the guidance of a master to collectively produce works of art. Such "factory art" was once the norm, before the rise of the individual artist during the Renaissance.

My point is that helping students learn how to balance independence with interdependence need not be approached merely as an isolated socialization exercise. Indeed, it would seem artificial to do so. Rather, socialization should take place in the normal contexts of teaching standard subject matter.

Rights and Responsibilities. Another general balance point concerns rights, both individual and group, and responsibilities, again both individual and group. Let's examine a concrete example:

Students in a fourth-grade class are required to keep a daily journal. This is an individual responsibility, but it is expected of all students. Eileen writes about what happens in her life. Some of what she writes is personal. When students are invited to share their journal entries, Eileen is embarrassed. How might the teacher and students cooperate to honor Eileen's right to privacy and still fulfill the expectations of the assignment, which is a group responsibility?

One strategy might be to allow all students to keep two-part journals: one part labeled "private," the other "public." Eileen can fulfill her individual journal-keeping responsibility and still maintain her right to privacy. When sharing time rolls around, Eileen can feel free — as can other students — to share only the "public" portion of her journal. At the same time, students also might discuss how to honor individual expressions: They should be responsible as a group for their behavior. Thus they might collectively determine a set of guidelines, such as thanking the individual for sharing his or her ideas, asking constructive questions, and responding without judging.

Again, while the teacher might direct students to these ends, the lesson will be learned at a deeper level if students discuss the issues and come to their own decisions under the teacher's guidance.

It should be evident from these examples that attaining balance in these three broad areas will require attention to two essential instructional strategies: collaboration and conflict resolution. Learning how to collaborate and how to resolve conflicts are life skills that implement the basic principles of community to which M. Scott Peck refers in his book, *The Different Drum: Community Making and Peace*, when he says:

> I am dubious . . . as to how far we can move toward global community — which is the only way to achieve international peace — until we learn the basic principles of community in our own lives and personal spheres of influence. (1987, pp. 17-18)

The next two sections of this chapter form a discussion of collaboration and conflict resolution in classroom settings. I take up the first in general terms because much has been written in other sources about strategies for cooperative learning and other forms of collaboration. The second, conflict resolution, is an element of collaboration. But it often is the most troublesome element. I believe it merits somewhat more attention. Thus the scenarios

120

that I will set forth in that section on conflict resolution are intended to offer ways to examine collaboration with particular attention to the aspect that most challenges the creativity, perspicacity, and perseverance of teachers and students.

Teaching Collaboration

Collaboration incorporates a number of "c" words: cooperation, communication, civility, common sense, and conflict resolution, to name but a few. It is synonymous with cooperative learning, popularized in recent years by Robert Slavin and his colleagues.

Briefly, cooperative learning is based on a prejudice-reduction theory advanced by Gordon Allport (1954). Allport's *contact thesis* posits that prejudice among individuals can be reduced if the individuals work together as equals on a common task over a sustained period. Subsequent research has demonstrated the validity of Allport's notion.

Robert Slavin and his colleagues at the Center for Social Organization of Schools at Johns Hopkins University tweaked Allport's contact thesis to focus on learning and interpersonal relationships. Slavin suggests that when students work together as equals toward a common learning goal, then their learning will increase as measured by standard tests of academic achievement *in addition to* the improvement in interpersonal relationships, which was the thrust of Allport's work. Slavin's research led him to conclude:

> For academic achievement, cooperative learning techniques are no worse than traditional techniques [based on competition] and in most cases they are significantly better. (1983, p. 429)

From the teacher's standpoint, cooperative learning is an active-learning approach to instruction. Students who are permitted to work with one another cannot sustain a passive role for long, as they might in a teacher-centered classroom. Once the general nature of cooperative learning is explained to students, the teacher then typically assigns students to four- or five-mem-

121

ber teams. In most cooperative learning situations the students are mixed — by ability (including students with disabilities), race, religion, sex, social class, and so on. This integration of "differences" helps to make cooperative learning a powerful strategy in teaching for diversity.

The student teams are provided with, or decide for themselves, the instructional objectives to be accomplished in the lesson at hand. Each member of the cooperative team will be expected to assist in the attainment of the group goals as well as to achieve his or her individual objectives. Assessment must follow this principle, too. Teachers must evaluate attainment of both group and individual objectives.

Cooperative learning tends to improve academic achievement for at least two reasons. First, students can draw on their strengths; often as group work is parceled out, students can play to their particular academic strengths and interests. The mural project that I described previously is an example of this feature in action. Second, student learning of new information is assisted by drawing on the strengths of others in the cooperative learning group. Students help one another in the acquisition of information and the construction of meaning through discussion, debate, and negotiation.

As students work on academic subject matter, they must communicate with one another: They must discuss ideas, share information, compromise, resolve conflicts. And all of this must be accomplished with civility, maintaining an acceptable level of classroom decorum. And so students in cooperative groups also work out differences and develop important social skills. They develop study relationships and friendships across lines of "difference," whether that difference is ability, race, sex, class, or some other factor.

Part of the power of cooperative learning is its immediacy. Students learn, in part, by teaching one another, which in turn encourages both interdependence and self-reliance. One student cannot always be "the teacher"; he or she must occasionally take the role of "the student," and vice versa. Well-structured cooper-

122

ative learning situations reduce students' sense of risk. Being "wrong" simply means that someone will help, someone in the group will know the right answer, and everyone will benefit — and no student will be wrong all the time.

I have painted the rosiest picture of cooperative learning. But, of course, successful collaboration does not just happen. It is learned. And a major part of learning to cooperate — beyond simple sharing and turn-taking — is learning how to resolve conflicts.

Conflict Resolution

To some extent, cooperation is natural. Most children beyond a certain age already know how to share, whether the item in question is a toy or an idea. Most children learn early about taking turns and playing together — and working together in a variety of ways. But with young children, conflicts are most often resolved by the parent, teacher, or someone in authority stepping in. The challenge in teaching for diversity — and specifically in using cooperative learning as an instructional strategy — is helping students learn how to solve problems and to resolve conflicts on their own, without the intervention of authority.

Many teachers shy away from the constructive use of conflict as a teaching tool. We dislike conflict, and so we are more inclined to step in and put an end to it, rather than to treat a conflict as a teachable moment. One advantage of using cooperative learning is that it helps students (and teachers) to understand 1) that conflicts are a natural consequence of human variation and 2) that conflicts can be resolved peaceably and, in so doing, will strengthen individual character and the cohesiveness of the group or community.

Furthermore, conflicts that arise in classrooms (as in the "real world") do not simply go away. Left unresolved, they fester like untreated sores. And so the most productive course for teachers and students is to tackle conflicts head on.

Following are some general guidelines that I will amplify with a series of scenarios. In using a conflict as a teaching opportunity, the teacher needs to help the students:

123

- Define the conflict as objectively as possible;
- Focus on the immediate problem without bringing up past problems, differences, or hostilities that will divert attention from solving the immediate conflict;
- Brainstorm possible resolutions, keeping in mind that, at first, any suggested solution should be recorded without judgment;
- Evaluate the suggested resolutions by identifying the common ground and isolating the conflict;
- Negotiate areas of difference through debate and compromise in order to arrive at consensus; and
- Set a resolution in place and determine when and how to evaluate its success.

The scenarios that follow are intended to show actual conflicts and how these general guidelines can be applied in specific situations. Each scenario portrays an actual incident from a classroom somewhere in Canada or the United States. The incidents were contributed by several graduate students with whom I have worked and who are teachers in public and private schools. Actual names and places are not used. My hope is that from these scenarios readers will find points of similarity to their own situations and generalizations that will fit their particular needs.

For the first three scenarios I have arranged the text to begin with a general precept. This statement of principle is followed by the case description itself. Readers who want to actively use these scenarios are then encouraged to take up four questions in relation to each case:

1. How is the case related to the precept? What is the intellectual context for the incident recounted in the scenario?
2. What is the problem or conflict (a specific definition) and whence does the conflict arise (specific sources)?
3. What sociocultural factors are at work in the conflict that must be addressed by any successful resolution?
4. How can the conflict be resolved? Are various resolutions possible?

Scenario #1

Precept: Respecting Cultural Differences

Respect for cultural differences requires teachers to be sensitive to the fact that others, including their students, may behave in ways that seem "odd" or simply "different" because of cultural variations. But those who seem "different" also have a right to their differences, to their cultures. Some cultural variations may not be visible at a glance. Therefore, rather than acting on their own cultural biases impulsively, teachers should delve behind the surface impression and strive for understanding before acting. In some cases, simply asking questions and listening carefully to the answers can avoid conflict.

"Juanita's Dirty Arm"

Teachers at a reservation school had been told to respect the culture of their Native American students, but they knew little of that culture. One day in a seventh-grade classroom the teacher, Mrs. Fonda, noticed that Juanita, normally a tidy youngster, had a brown smear of dirt on one arm. That day and the next, Mrs. Fonda said nothing about the smear, but when Juanita came a third day with the smear, Mrs. Fonda could not be silent.

"Juanita, go wash your dirty arm," she said.

"It's not dirty," responded Juanita.

"It looks dirty to me."

"But I've got to. . . ," started Juanita.

"Don't argue with me," interrupted Mrs. Fonda sternly. "I'm the teacher here. Do what you're told!"

Juanita left the classroom mumbling, but she complied with Mrs. Fonda's command. Two days later, Juanita was taken out of school by her parents to attend the funeral of her sister. After two weeks she had not returned, and so the principal visited her home to ask why. Here is what Juanita's mother said:

"In our way, when someone in the family is ill, each of us places a spot of oil and soil somewhere on our body. We are one with nature. Illness is a sign that we are out of balance with nature. We use the oil and soil of our Mother, the earth, to show that we wish our sick one to be in balance with nature.

125

"When the teacher made Juanita wash her arm, she broke our oneness with nature. That is why her sister died. The teacher caused her death. She is bad for Juanita and for our family. Juanita cannot go back to class with Mrs. Fonda."

Scenario #2

Precept: Recognizing Cultural Relativism

Cultural relativism is a concept defined by anthropologists as a nonjudgmental approach to understanding cultures different from our own. For example, Native Americans were described by early white settlers as "primitives," because the white settlers saw them in relation to their own European culture, which they believed to be more advanced and refined. From a perspective of cultural relativism, the culture of a Native American tribe or community is neither "primitive" nor "advanced," except in accordance with its own, internal cultural standards.

"Myth or Truth?"

During a unit on ethnic literature, the teacher assigned a reading about a Native American creation myth. In brief that reading went as follows:

> "That Which Knows and Does Everything" (WKDE) lived above the sky with a daughter. One day the daughter fell through a hole in the sky. An eagle caught her and placed her on the back of a large turtle. Other turtles gathered mud from the ocean bottom. Soon a great island existed. The eagle brought grass and twigs from far away. They grew. WKDE asked the daughter to return. She refused and said she wanted to stay on the ground. WKDE granted her wish. Then she had a son. Soon the whole island was filled with people. That is how the first Indians were created."

When various students' parents became aware of the reading, several voiced objections to the assignment. They objected on grounds that:

- The story taught that there might be more than one God.

126

- The story taught strange ideas about God, such as WKDE had no gender.
- WKDE created a woman before creating a man.
- The story raised a question about who the father of the daughter's son might be.

The teacher responded that the American Indian myth left many questions unanswered, as did the creation myth in the Bible. The parents countered angrily that the biblical story of creation was truth, not myth.

Scenario #3

Precept: Discerning Causes of Racial Prejudice

Prejudice is learned, but such learning may arise from many sources. One source may be a belief in racial superiority. If an individual believes that his or her race is superior to other races, then those of another race must be inferior. Another source may be remembered injury. If an individual has been injured — physically, psychologically, economically, or in some other way — by an individual of another race, the injured person may generalize ill feelings toward all members of that race. Yet another source may be a belief in racial stereotypes. If an individual generalizes that persons of another race all hold beliefs contrary to his or her own or all behave in ways that the individual considers to be wrong, then that individual may see everyone of that race in a negative way. These are only three possible sources of prejudice.

Prejudice often is expressed in ignorance. Individuals may use language that persons of another race will find to be pejorative or insulting, though the user intends no disparagement. Prejudicial statements can as often be naive as they are calculated. While it may be difficult to do, discerning the sources of prejudice or the use of prejudicial language can be a first step toward eliminating racial prejudice.

"A 'Big Deal' Over One Word"

Lumbermen and others in the small British Columbia town commonly used the term "boy" to mean a person who is adept at getting what he wants. The Wilsons, an African-American family, moved from Atlanta to the northern town so that Mr. Wilson could assist in automating the local timber mill. They were the first black family ever to live there.

Leroy, the Wilsons' seventh-grade son, attended the local school. Although he was gregarious and a good athlete, some students complained that he was "pushy" and "liked to argue a lot." One day, Leroy was sent home by the principal, who wrote to the Wilsons:

> Leroy is his own worst enemy. His classmates have bent over backwards to be nice to him, but he returns their friendship by arguing about almost everything. Leroy has been suspended from school because he provoked a fight during a volleyball game. Before he will be readmitted to school, he must apologize to Russ Schmidt, his classmate, for hitting him hard enough to cause a nosebleed and a black eye.

Leroy admitted to his parents that he had beaten up Russ Schmidt. He complained: "I wish we were back in Atlanta, where I was just one of the guys. Everyone here makes a big deal about my being black. Sure, they're just joking when they ask, 'Will your chocolate skin melt in the summer?' One girl asked how she could have a 'kinky' hairdo like mine. So when Russ kept calling me 'cool boy,' I got mad. They were all calling me 'boy.' I couldn't take it. It may be only one word, but it's a big deal to me."

These three scenarios offer opportunities to discuss the four questions I suggested previously. The next two scenarios are wider ranging, and so I have omitted the precept statement. Readers may wish to consider them in relation to a mix of concepts that I have presented in the course of this book, such as ethnocentrism, assimilation, integration, and so on. The four questions remain pertinent; however, the first question should be adapted: What are the precepts at work in the scenario?

I call Scenario #4 "A Time and Place for Everything." It should raise questions about the role of the school in students' personal lives. Should the school merely reflect a student's culture? Or, to phrase the question from a different viewpoint, should the school merely allow the student free expression of his or her home culture? Or should the school seek to enlarge that culture, to change the student's perspective?

Scenario #4

"A Time and Place for Everything"

Sally Monroe is an eighth-grade math teacher. She takes justifiable pride in her ability to motivate her students. She uses a contract system. The more a student does, the higher his or her grade will be. To earn an A, B, or C, a student must do some homework.

In spite of having done well in sixth-grade math, Frankie Valdez always contracts for a D — no homework. Mrs. Monroe has written several notes home, explaining that Frankie is a bright student capable of higher achievement, but they have made no difference. One day, Mrs. Monroe runs into Frankie's mother in the grocery store.

Mrs. Monroe: Hello, Mrs. Valdez. How nice to see you. I must tell you that Frankie is a delight to have in class. He never fools around, and he is always very respectful. When I give him an assignment, he makes sure it is done correctly.

Mrs. Valdez: We have taught him to respect his teachers. He will not give you any trouble.

Mrs. Monroe: Did he show you the notes I sent home.

Mrs. Valdez: Oh, yes. We read them.

Mrs. Monroe: Frankie has such a high aptitude in math, but he only does the minimum to get by. Is he a lazy boy at home?

Mrs. Valdez: Not at all. In fact, he's very good at fixing things around the house.

Mrs. Monroe: Then, why. . . ?

Mrs. Valdez: It is wrong that you give homework. There is a time and place for everything. My husband works hard and so do I. We don't fool around at work. The day is for work, and the night is for rest and doing what needs to be done at home.

Mrs. Monroe: But don't you want Frankie to be successful? to get a good job? He could do very well with his math skills. . . .

Mrs. Valdez: There's nothing wrong with what my husband and I do for a living — and we believe our family life is as important as what the school may do.

Scenario #5

"Cutting Paper Dolls"

Hank Reynolds' classes were always lively. A tenth-grade English teacher, Mr. Reynolds encouraged his students to "read between the lines," to seek deeper meaning instead of just settling for the obvious in the stories they read. One day, when the class had finished reading a series of short stories on the theme of women's liberation, he began to probe how the various stories portrayed the women protagonists' quests for freedom from male domination and oppression.

Mr. Reynolds: How were these stories different from one another?

Sue: Different settings, places.

Jean: Different times in history.

Beth: Different topics, like being rich — or poor.

Mr. Reynolds: Good. Now, how were the stories similar to one another?

Sue: Well, every story was about minorities.

Adam: Huh? The stories were all about how guys are mean to women.

Sue: But, Mr. Reynolds, women are minorities, right?

Adam: Look, we learned in biology that there are always more females than males in every species. Women can't be minorities because there are more of them than men.

Mr. Reynolds: Let's get back to the similarities. What are some others?

Adam: All the villains in the stories are guys!

Jean: That's not true. What about the guy in the Faulkner story?

Adam: Sure, he wasn't bad. He was just crazy.

And so the discussion went, with Adam defending the male viewpoint. Later, the class was divided into groups to construct collages from magazine clippings, which would portray the protagonists' struggles. Mr. Reynolds reasoned that the assignment would offer students a creative way to demonstrate their understanding of the themes of the stories. Adam worked for a while, then he threw up his arms in protest: "This stinks! Cutting paper dolls is women's work. I won't do it!" And with that, he snatched up his group's collage, tore it to pieces, and threw it on the floor.

This last scenario raises a number of diversity issues related to sex and gender. It also illustrates a cooperative learning activity gone awry, apparently because of a stereotypical prejudice. But there may be more at work beneath the surface. Applying the four questions I posed earlier can be a useful strategy.

While these scenarios and others like them are useful to stimulate reflection and discussion, they also may serve as jumping off points for creative conflict resolution when actual conflicts arise in the classroom. Students might write their own scenarios based on conflicts they have experienced. Or the scenarios might be used to model role-playing, which could lead to the creation of original scenarios to be acted out by students as they learn how to resolve conflicts of various kinds.

Conclusion

In this chapter my goal has been to bring together the themes of the preceding chapters and to give them a slightly different spin. Teaching for diversity has two distinct but closely related thrusts. The first, with which I have been most concerned in Chapters One through Four, is teaching *about* diversity — that is, helping students and teachers to become aware of diversity characteristics through sensitivity to issues, instruction, and curricula. The second thrust of teaching *for* diversity is helping students learn how to live in a diverse society. This theme is imbedded in the first four chapters, but I have tried to tackle it directly in this chapter. I have suggested that socialization to diversity in the classroom will help to socialize students to diversity in the society outside the school.

No one knows exactly what the future holds, but one thing seems certain: Diversity will be a fact of life in the 21st century. Of course, human diversity has always existed, however much it has been ignored or minimized or subordinated. The emergence of the information age simply has made — or will make — everyone more aware of human "differences." My hope is that human variations will come to be seen universally as things to be prized. Multiculturalism is, at heart, about valuing *all* cultures, not about determining which will dominate, which will be elite, and which will be inferior.

Educators will be ever more challenged in years to come to help students understand the human variations in the world around them. They cannot confine teaching merely to the diversity represented among the students in their individual classrooms — though some classrooms of students may be very diverse indeed. Rather, teachers must look to the global diversity of a world being shrunk by advanced technology, particularly in communication and transportation. Today's students are not merely citizens of their classroom "village" or even of their town or nation; they are citizens of the world.

As world citizens, students in today's classrooms also need to study the issues raised by diversity. Tolerance and acceptance of diversity are stronger when undergirded by awareness and sensitivity. Students need to acquire knowledge about aspects of diversity, such as ethnicity, race, class, sex, gender, sexual orientation, religion, and ability. Such knowledge will be most effectively acquired not in isolated culture studies but in context — as students work independently and interdependently; as they study the subject matter of history, literature, the arts, science, and mathematics; and as they learn how to resolve conflicts.

Famed physicist Albert Einstein said:

> Something more is needed to produce a truly educated person — namely, an ever-present feeling of social responsibility for one's fellow human being. . . . If [teachers] are able to teach young people to have a critical mind and a socially oriented attitude, they will have done all that is necessary. (1968, p. 310)

"A critical mind and a socially oriented attitude" capture well the substance of this book. Teaching for diversity, as I hope that I have demonstrated, consists of a complex of related strategies that, taken as a whole, will help teachers engender in their students a capacity for critical thinking, especially about social issues — for analyzing issues of cultural diversity, appearances, language, and situations; for weighing information against values and beliefs, observations and stereotypes; for synthesizing knowledge and creating meaning; and for evaluating diversity without prejudice. These skills are critical for success today and in the new century ahead. They are important in school and in the world outside the school.

References

Addams, Jane. *Democracy and Social Ethics*. New York: Macmillan, 1907.

Adler, Mortimer J. *The Paideia Proposal: An Educational Manifesto*. New York: Macmillan, 1982.

Ai-Ling, Louie. *Yeh Shen: A Cinderella Story from China*. New York: Philomel, 1982.

Allport, Gordon. *The Nature of Prejudice*. Cambridge, Mass.: Addison-Wesley, 1954.

Anyon, Jean. "Social Class and the Hidden Curriculum of Work." In *School and Society*, edited by Jeanne Ballantine. Mountain View, Calif.: Mayfield, 1989.

Au, Kathryn H. *Literacy Instruction in Multicultural Settings*. Fort Worth: Harcourt Brace Jovanovich, 1993.

Banks, James A. *The Canon Debate: Knowledge Construction and Multicultural Education*. New York: Teachers College Press, 1996.

Banks, James A. *Multicultural Education: Issues and Perspectives*. Boston: Allyn & Bacon, 1989.

Bell, A., and Weinberg, M. *Homosexualities: A Study of Diversity Among Men and Women*. Bloomington: Indiana University Press, 1981.

Benedict, Ruth. *Patterns of Culture*. Boston: Houghton Mifflin, 1934.

Bernstein, Basil. "A Sociolinguistic Approach to Socialization." In *Language and Poverty*, edited by F. Williams. Chicago: Markham, 1970.

Blumfeld, Warren J. *Homophobia: How We All Pay the Price*. Boston: Beacon Press, 1992.

Bowles, Samuel, and Gintis, Herbert. *Schooling in Capitalist America*. New York: Basic Books, 1976.

Byrnes, James. *Cognitive Development and Learning*. Boston: Allyn and Bacon, 1996.

Cabeza de Baca, Fabiola. *We Fed Them Cactus*. Albuquerque: University of New Mexico Press, 1954.

Cazden, Courtney. *Classroom Discourse*. Portsmouth, N.H.: Heinemann, 1988.

Cummins, Jim. "An Analysis of Programmes and Practices in Ontario." In *Minority Education*, edited by T. Skutnabb-Kangas and Jim Cummins. Clevendon, England: Multilingual Matters, 1988.

Cushner, Kenneth; McClelland, Averil; and Safford, Philip. *Human Diversity in Education: An Integrative Approach*. New York: McGraw-Hill, 1992.

DeStefano, A. "NY Teens Anti-Gay Poll Findings." *Newsday*, 10 May 1988, p. 3.

Dewey, John. *Experience and Education*. New York: Macmillan, 1938.

Dewey, John. *How We Think*. Lexington, Ky.: D.C. Heath, 1933.

Diaz, Carlos. *Multicultural Education for the 21st Century*. Washington, D.C.: National Education Association, 1992.

Du Bois, W.E.B. *The Soul of Black Folks: Essays and Sketches*. Chicago: A.C. McClurg, 1903.

Dudley, Joseph Iron Eye. *Choteau Creek*. Lincoln: University of Nebraska Press, 1992.

Einstein, Albert. "On Education: A Speech to the New Jersey Education Association." In *Einstein on Peace*, edited by Otto Nathan and Heinz Norden. New York: Schocken, 1968.

Fishman, Joshua. *Language Loyalty in the United States*. The Hague: Mouton, 1966.

Flax, Ellen. "Special Problems of Homosexual Students." *Education Week*, 7 January 1990, p. 2.

Freire, Paulo. *Pedagogy of the Oppressed*. New York: Seabury Press, 1970.

Friesen, John W. *When Cultures Clash*. Calgary: Detselig, 1993.

Garcia, Eugene. *Early Childhood Bilingualism*. Albuquerque: University of New Mexico Press, 1983.

Garcia, Ricardo L. *Education for Cultural Pluralism: Global Roots Stew*. Fastback 159. Bloomington, Ind.: Phi Delta Kappa Educational Foundation, 1981.

Gardner, Howard, and Hatch, T. "Multiple Intelligences Go to School." *Educational Researcher* 18 (November 1989): 4-10.

Gay, Geneva. *At the Essence of Learning: Multicultural Education.* West Lafayette, Ind.: Kappa Delta Pi, 1994.

Gay, Geneva. "Culturally Diverse Students and Social Studies." In *Handbook of Research on Social Studies Teaching and Learning,* edited by J.P. Shaver. New York: Macmillan, 1991.

Gay, Geneva. "On Behalf of Children: A Curriculum Design for Multicultural Education in the Elementary School." *Journal of Negro Education* 38 (Summer 1979): 324-40.

Gay, Geneva. "Differential Dyadic Interactions of Black and White Teachers with Black and White Pupils in Recently Desegregated Social Studies Classrooms: A Function of Teacher and Pupil Ethnicity." OE Project no. 2Fl 13, January 1974.

Gies, Frances, and Gies, Joseph. *Life in a Medieval Village.* New York: Harper & Row, 1990.

Good, Thomas L. "Teacher Expectations and Student Perception." *Educational Leadership* 38 (February 1981): 415-42.

Goodlad, John I. *A Place Called School.* New York: McGraw-Hill, 1984.

Gould, Stephen Jay. *The Mismeasure of Man.* New York: W.W. Norton, 1981.

Harbeck, Karen M. *Coming Out of the Classroom Closet.* New York: Harrington Park Press, 1991.

Hart, Betty, and Risley, Todd. *Meaningful Differences in the Everyday Experience of Young Children.* Baltimore: Brookes, 1995.

Herrnstein, Richard J., and Murray, Charles. *The Bell Curve: Intelligence and Class Structure in American Life.* New York: Free Press, 1994.

Hetrick, Emery S., and Martin, A. Damien. *Developmental Issues and Their Resolution for Gay and Lesbian Adolescents.* New York: Haworth Press, 1987.

House of Commons. *Bill C-93. An Act for the Preservation and Enhancement of Multiculturalism in Canada.* Passed 12 July 1988.

Hunter, John Davidson. *Culture Wars: The Struggle to Define America.* New York: Basic Books, 1991.

Jensen, A.R. "How Can We Boost IQ and Scholastic Achievement?" *Harvard Educational Review* 39 (Winter 1969): 1-123.

Katz, Michael. *Class, Bureaucracy and the Schools.* New York: Praeger, 1976.

Kozol, Jonathan. *Savage Inequalities: Children in America's Schools.* New York: Crown, 1991.

Lambert, Wallace, and Tucker, Richard. *Bilingual Education of Children: The Saint Lambert Experiment*. Rowley, Mass.: Newbury, 1972.

Maccoby, Eleanor E., and Jacklin, Carol. *Psychology of Sex Difference*. Palo Alto, Calif.: Stanford University Press, 1974.

Maccoby, Eleanor E., and Martin, John A. "Socialization in the Context of the Family." In *Handbook of Child Psychology*, edited by E.M. Hetherington. New York: John Wiley & Sons, 1983.

McLuhan, Marshall, and Powers, Bruce R. *The Global Village*. New York: Oxford University Press, 1989.

Macnamara, John. "Cognitive Basis of Language Learning in Infants." *Psychological Review* 79 (January 1972): 1-13.

Murillo, Nathan. "George I. Sanchez and Mexican American Educational Practices." In *Transformative Knowledge and Action*, edited by James A. Banks. New York: Teachers College Press, 1996.

National Council for the Accreditation of Teacher Education. "Teachers in Demographic Denial." *Quality Teaching, The Newsletter of NCATE* 5 (Spring 1996): 4.

Neill, A.S. *Summerhill: A Radical Approach to Child Rearing*. New York: Hart, 1960.

Oakes, Jeannie. *Keeping Track: How Schools Structure Inequality*. New Haven, Conn.: Yale University Press, 1985.

Ogbu, John. "Class Stratification, Racial Stratification, and Schooling." In *Race, Class, and Schooling*, edited by L. Weis. Buffalo: State University of New York Press, 1986.

Parker, Franklin. *George I. Sanchez, 1906-1972, Texas Educator*. Private printing. Morgantown: West Virginia University, May 1972.

Paul, Richard. *Critical Thinking*. Santa Rosa, Calif.: Foundation for Critical Thinking, 1993.

Peck, M. Scott. *The Different Drum: Community Making and Peace*. New York: Simon and Schuster, 1987.

Phillips, Susan. *The Invisible Culture: Communication in Classroom and Community on the Warm Springs Indian Reservation*. New York: Longman, 1983.

Qoyawayma, Polingaysi. *No Turning Back*. Albuquerque: University of New Mexico Press, 1964.

Reyhner, Jon. *Teaching American Indian Students*. Norman: University of Oklahoma Press, 1992.

Rice, Mabel L. "Children's Language Acquisition." *American Psychologist* 44 (February 1989): 149-56.

Rosenthal, Robert, and Rubin, Donald. "Interpersonal Expectancy Effects." *Behavioral and Brain Sciences* 5, no. 3 (1976): 414-20.

Sanchez, George I. *The Forgotten People*. Albuquerque: University of New Mexico Press, 1940.

Schrag, Francis. *Thinking in School and Society*. New York: Routledge, 1988.

Shor, Ira. *Empowering Education*. Chicago: University of Chicago Press, 1992.

Sium, Bairu. "Streaming in Education and Beyond: Students Talk." In *Multicultural and Intercultural Education: Building Canada*, edited by Sonia V. Morris. Calgary: Detselig, 1989.

Slavin, Robert. *Educational Psychology: Theory and Practice*. 5th ed. Boston: Allyn & Bacon, 1994.

Slavin, Robert. "Synthesis on Research in Cooperative Learning." *Educational Leadership* 48 (February 1991): 71-82.

Slavin, Robert. "When Does Cooperative Learning Increase Student Achievement?" *Psychological Bulletin* 94 (November 1983): 429-45.

Snyderman, Mark, and Rothman, Stanley. "Survey on Expert Opinion on Intelligence and Aptitude Testing." *American Psychologist* 42 (February 1987): 137-44.

Spring, Joel. *The Sorting Machine Revisited*. New York: Longman, 1989.

Steptoe, John. *Mufaro's Beautiful Daughters*. New York: Lothrop, Lee, Shephard, 1987.

U.S. Commission on Civil Rights. *Teachers and Students*. Washington, D.C.: U.S. Government Printing Office, 1973.

Uribe, Virginia. "Homophobia: What It Is and Who It Hurts." *Project 10 Handbook*. Los Angeles: Friends of Projects 10, 1989.

Whitlock, K. *Bridges of Respect: Creating Support for Lesbian and Gay Youth*. Philadelphia: American Friends Service, 1989.

Willis, Paul . *Learning to Labor*. Lexington, Ky.: D.C. Heath, 1977.

Wilson, Edward O. *On Human Nature*. Cambridge, Mass.: Harvard University Press, 1978.

Woolfolk, Anita. *Educational Psychology*. 6th ed. Boston: Allyn & Bacon, 1995.

About the Author

Ricardo L Garcia is a professor of education at Teachers College at the University of Nebraska-Lincoln. He also is on the lecture circuit as a Hispanic storyteller.

Garcia began his education career in 1963 as a high school English and history teacher in northern New Mexico. Since then he has continuously served in classrooms as a teacher, consultant, storyteller, and college professor.

In 1973, Garcia became a co-director for a Desegregation Teacher Training institute at Kansas State University. Since then, he has conducted research and taught about education for students in a diverse, democratic society. Garcia has given his cross-cultural instructional theories practical tests by teaching on Indian reservations and in state penitentiaries. He also has administered diversity programming at the University of Wisconsin-Stevens Point and the University of Nebraska.

Garcia is the author of three Phi Delta Kappa fastbacks: 84 *Learning in Two Languages* (also published in Spanish), 107 *Fostering a Pluralistic Society Through Multi-Ethnic Education*, and 159 *Education for Cultural Pluralism: Global Roots Stew*. He is an active member of Phi Delta Kappa International and has served in a number of chapter offices. He also has conducted numerous presentations throughout the United States, including Puerto Rico, as part of the Phi Delta Kappa Educational Foundation seminar-lecture series.